W9-BEQ-379

scams!

•••

true stories from the edge

Andreas Schroeder

true stories from the edge

scams!

Ten stories that explore some of the most outrageous swindlers and tricksters of all time

ANNICK PRESS

TORONTO + NEW YORK + VANCOUVER

© 2004 by Andreas Schroeder

Annick Press Ltd.

All rights reserved. No part of this work covered by the copyrights hereon may be reproduced or used in any form or by any means — graphic, electronic, or mechanical — without the prior written permission of the publisher.

We acknowledge the support of the Canada Council for the Arts, the Ontario Arts Council, the Government of Ontario through the Ontario Book Publishers Tax Credit program and the Ontario Book Initiative, and the Government of Canada through the Book Publishing Industry Development Program (BPIDP) for our publishing activities.

The author gratefully acknowledges the support of the British Columbia Arts Council.

Edited by Pam Robertson
Copy-edited by Elizabeth McLean
Cover art by Scott Cameron
Design by Irvin Cheung/iCheung Design

Cataloging in Publication Data
Schroeder, Andreas, 1946–
      Scams! / by Andreas Schroeder.

(True stories from the edge)
Includes bibliographical references and index.
ISBN 1-55037-853-8 (bound).--ISBN 1-55037-852-X (pbk.)
      1. Fraud--Juvenile literature. 2. Swindlers and swindling--Juvenile literature. I. Title.
II. Series.

HV6691.S339 2004   j364.16'3   C2003-906474-3

The text was typeset in Bembo.

Distributed in Canada by	Distributed in the U.S.A. by	Published in the U.S.A. by
Firefly Books Ltd.	Firefly Books (U.S.) Inc.	Annick Press (U.S.) Ltd.
66 Leek Crescent	P.O. Box 1338	
Richmond Hill, ON	Ellicott Station	
L4B 1H1	Buffalo, NY 14205	

Printed and bound in Canada by Friesens, Altona, Manitoba

Visit us at **www.annickpress.com**

Contents

What Are Scams, Anyway?

IN 1916, an American inventor named Louis Enricht announced that he had discovered a cheap additive that turned ordinary tap water into automotive fuel. At a time when World War I was raging in Europe and gasoline was selling for a whopping 30 cents a gallon, Enricht claimed that his additive would bring the per-gallon cost down to a single penny.

That certainly got everyone's attention.

Enricht let a crowd of reporters check that his jug was full of ordinary tap water, then poured in a small amount of greenish liquid, stirred it up, and invited everyone to test this miraculous mixture in their own vehicles.

They did—and it worked!

Enricht's demonstrations were so convincing that even the world-famous automaker Henry Ford offered him millions to buy the rights for his additive.

Actually, Enricht had merely discovered that if you add a very cheap chemical called acetone to water it will run an engine—for a while. Then it will destroy it. But before anyone found that out, Enricht had managed to convince not only Henry Ford, but several other famous American businessmen who should have known better, to give him millions of dollars for his worthless invention.

So Enricht's claim was too good to be true, and that is one of the main characteristics of scams. Another is money. Most scam artists invent scams to fool their victims into giving them money—though it doesn't always have to be that. It can also be something else of great value, such as love or power or fame.

Whenever we hear or read about a scam, our first reaction is often: "How could those people have let themselves be fooled so easily? How could they have been so stupid?"

Good question. It would make sense if only stupid people fell for scams—but they don't. Perfectly intelligent people fall for scams too. People like you and me.

So what is it that makes perfectly intelligent people shut off their brains and fall for crooks like Louis Enricht?

Sometimes it's just greed. The tantalizing chance to get something for nothing. It's one of the oldest motivators of humankind. And here we're talking about both the scam artists *and* their victims. Most scams wouldn't work if the victim weren't a little greedy too.

Oscar Hartzell, a poor farm boy from Iowa, understood that very well when he cooked up the idea of contacting everyone in the United States whose surname was Drake. He told them he'd made an astonishing discovery: due to a bureaucratic bungle, the estate of the famous British pirate Sir Francis Drake had never been paid out to his heirs. It had just been sitting there for over 300 years, gathering interest. So by now it was worth an eye-popping *four trillion dollars*—enough money to buy all of England, Scotland, Ireland, and Wales combined! Hartzell invited Drakes from all over North America to invest in his campaign to take the British government to court to retrieve that money. He promised that everyone would make at least $500 for every dollar invested.

You wouldn't believe how many people fell for that scam. Not just thousands—*tens* of thousands. Housewives sent Hartzell their grocery money. Kids sent him their allowance. Retirees sent him their life savings. Some ministers even sent him their church donations! The former farmer's boy from Iowa was able to move to England, become a duke, and live like a king in a mansion with maids, cooks, butlers, gardeners, and drivers. Even after the FBI checked out his story and announced that it was a total lie, that Sir Francis Drake's wife had inherited and duly received her husband's estate back in 1597, people kept sending Hartzell their money. Even after Hartzell was arrested, tried, and sent to Leavenworth Penitentiary, people *still* kept sending him their cash. They didn't stop until he finally died, in prison, after operating his scam for over 30 years.

Hard to believe? Some people say, well, that was 1913, people weren't so sophisticated then. But I don't see much evidence of that. Consider some of the scams that operate through e-mail and the Internet today. There's the famous "Nigerian Letter," for example, that people have been receiving via e-mail for the past several years. In it, a wife or close relative of a Nigerian politician informs you that her husband managed to smuggle a vast fortune out of the country before his recent death. If you will help, she will give you a quarter (25 percent) of that fortune for your trouble.

If you reply, you'll be informed that the money is being held by a "security company" that will give you the fortune if you'll pay them an administrative fee of $2,000. If you send them this fee, they'll request a customs fee, a notarization fee, a clearance fee, and on and on—as long as they can keep stringing you along.

According to the police, thousands of people get taken in by this kind of scam every year. In fact, the Nigerian letter is merely the latest version of what used to be called "The Spanish Letter." Believe it or not, there are historical references to this scam that go back over 400 years.

So greed accounts for a significant percentage of successful scams. But scams also pop up very reliably whenever there's a great *need* for something. Scams thrive on need and desperation. Let's say you borrowed someone's guitar and lost it, and it will cost hundreds of dollars to replace. How would you respond if someone offered to get you a replacement for, say, a mere 20 dollars? Or if you've always dreamed of a) being more popular, b) looking better, or c) being more successful, do you feel tempted by magazine advertisements promising to give you all that and more—*if* you'll just buy miraculous products that contain SECRET ingredients?

The people who fall for these sorts of scams aren't more or less intelligent than those who are merely greedy. They do so because they badly need this solution to be true. They're willing to put all their hope and money on the tiny possibility that they might—maybe, possibly—get what's promised.

I got caught in a scam myself in my twenties, when I threw my clothes and manuscripts into my truck and headed for the bright lights of Toronto. (That's where publishers were going to fall all over themselves in their eagerness to publish my work.) About a day's drive from Toronto I skidded through a corner and drove off the highway into the ditch.

The small-town mechanic to whose garage I was towed looked at my mangled truck and shook his head. "I suppose we could fix it," he said. "But I can get you a much newer truck for half the price." He explained that a friend of his worked for a business that repossessed automobiles, which it then auctioned off. "For peanuts," he assured me. "You wouldn't believe the deals I can get. The company doesn't care—it just wants to unload those vehicles fast."

But there was a catch. (There's always a catch with a scam.)

To buy at this auction, you had to pay for the vehicle on the spot, and my mechanic friend had little cash to spare. He suggested I leave him my truck and a cheque for $1,000. That would get me a near-new pickup at the next auction, whenever it happened. In the meantime he'd start to work on my old truck. If by some chance he couldn't get me that newer truck, I could apply the $1,000 to the repair of my old one.

Now it wasn't that I couldn't see the risks in this arrangement. I saw them quite clearly. But the mechanic seemed trustworthy. Later on, after many phone calls that produced neither a new truck nor my repaired old one (which ended up stripped in the back of the garage yard), I had to face the facts. I had been made gullible by my urgent wish to reverse my own bad luck. The garage mechanic had understood that, and had taken advantage of it. I really had no one to blame but myself.

An urgent need, or the desire to reverse bad luck, forms the basis for a number of stories in this collection. Desperate for his father's love and approval, a young man in England resorts to an extraordinary ruse to win it back. Faced with a leaky and malfunctioning boat, a yacht race contestant in the middle of the Atlantic Ocean decides to solve his problem in an ingenious fashion. Dogged by a criminal record that has ruined his career, a former teaching assistant in 19th-century Germany discovers a novel and unbelievably successful way to make a comeback.

Not all scams are amusing, but the best of them are totally fascinating. The 10 stories included here explore some of the most inventive and outrageous scams of all time. I was certainly amazed when I discovered them, and I'm sure you will be too!

The Tasaday: Stone-Age Cavemen of the Philippines

EARLY IN AUGUST 1971, a helicopter took off from Davao Airport on Mindanao Island in the southern Philippines, carrying four passengers and two crew. Its flight plan was vague—the pilot merely informed the control tower that they were headed "southwest" into the island's interior. Only powerful government officials could get away with keeping their flight plans secret. This helicopter was under the command of Manuel Elizalde Jr., head of the Philippine Ministry for National Minorities, and a close personal friend of Philippine President Marcos himself.

Wearing his trademark crumpled white yachting cap at a jaunty angle, Elizalde looked almost bored, but the other passengers—an American journalist and two American cameramen working for the National Geographic Society—could barely contain their excitement. They were going to be the first to document one of the most astonishing discoveries of the 20th century.

A month earlier, the Philippine government had made a stunning announcement: one of its agents had stumbled across a small tribe of 27 primitive cavemen, hidden deep in the Mindanao jungle.

Known as the Tasaday (taw-saw-day), these 7 men, 6 women, and 14 children were still living in caves as their ancestors had done thousands of years ago. They had never ventured out to the coast, had never encountered modern society, and still used only stone and bamboo tools. They wore loincloths made of leaves or grass, didn't hunt or fish, and ate only foods they could gather—wild fruit, yams, tadpoles or frogs, palm pith, and worms.

The news caused an uproar all over the world. This was like being able to travel back all the way to the Stone Age without using a time machine.

The find was especially exciting for the world's anthropologists and paleontologists—scientists who spent their careers trying to unlock the secrets of how our ancestors lived and evolved. Without live ancestors to talk to, they had to piece history together by patiently examining little bits of bone and fossils and trying to imagine how people and animals back then had looked and functioned. The process involved a lot of guesswork and could be very frustrating, because you could never really be sure your assumptions were right. So the opportunity to talk to 27 living, breathing cavemen still living exactly like our ancestors lived was simply mind-blowing.

Needless to say, the Philippine government was swamped with requests to meet, interview, photograph, and study the Tasaday. The requests came not only from scientists, but also from many newspaper and television journalists.

A lot of journalists didn't even bother trying to get permission. They just threw some clothes into a bag and grabbed the next available flight to Davao Airport, hoping to hire local guides to take them to the Tasaday.

Many of them had no idea what they were up against. The Tasaday caves were hidden in a mostly unmapped part of southwestern Mindanao. To get there by land you had to bounce and skid and plow your way through long stretches of rainforest by jeep, over very rough logging roads. These roads ended in small villages at the edge of the jungle, after which you still had to spend another week hacking and smashing your way through the jungle's almost impenetrable tangle of vines and brush.

Even if you managed to get that far, there was a final obstacle to overcome—an army of native warriors hired by Manuel Elizalde Jr. to keep people from getting into the Tasaday's territory.

Elizalde had made it clear that he wasn't about to have the Tasaday overrun by anybody—not loggers, not miners, and not western scientists or journalists. Anybody who wanted the privilege of studying the Tasaday had to file a proper petition, then get in line and wait. Elizalde said that the petitions would be evaluated on the basis of their scientific value and importance to humanity.

This concern was something about Elizalde that a lot of people found hard to understand. Elizalde was the son of a rich and influential Philippine family. Until a few years before he had never shown the slightest interest in native issues—or, for that matter, any selfless causes. He was very smart and could be very charming, but he could also be aggressive, rude, and careless. He drank a lot and was known as a party animal. A lot of people felt he'd been given his government appointment mostly because of his many political friends.

At the same time, he'd surprised people. Even though his family owned large mining and logging companies in the Philippines, he'd come out strongly against the invasion by such companies into areas inhabited not just by the Tasaday, but by native tribes all over the Philippines.

What everybody agreed on was that Elizalde liked money. Lots of money. Truckloads of money. He spent it recklessly. He was always roaring around in government helicopters and expensive jeeps. His ministry always seemed to be on the verge of bankruptcy, and some people said it was because Elizalde spent its money like a drunken sailor. (His crumpled white yachting cap didn't help that image.)

And then there was the preservation fund. Within days of announcing the discovery of the Tasaday, Elizalde established a Tasaday Preservation Fund that immediately began accepting donations. Even though Elizalde had said that access to the Tasaday would be judged on scientific value, it quickly became obvious that he was using a different measure—the size of one's donation. Somehow, if you couldn't afford to give a big donation, the scientific value of your petition quickly faded away.

Scientists and academics without a lot of money couldn't get their phone calls returned. Even scientists and journalists who actually lived in the Philippines were being ignored.

On the other hand, donations reportedly ranging from a quarter of a million to half a million dollars from rich television networks like America's NBC and Germany's NDR, and from newspaper and magazine publishers like *The New York Times, Life Magazine,* and *National Geographic,* quickly moved these petitioners to the head of the line.

Back in the helicopter, the Americans watched the jungle stretching like a solid green carpet on all sides. It was so densely treed that they couldn't imagine where the helicopter might land. About an hour after take-off the pilot began checking his instruments more often, and a few minutes later he put the aircraft into a steep dive. Soon they were hovering directly above the trees—and that's when the journalists realized how they were going to "land."

Bulldozing a clearing for a helicopter pad would have been a dead giveaway for the Tasaday's location, so Elizalde had brought in a team of Tboli natives with ropes and chainsaws to build a cunningly hidden landing platform—right in the top of an oak tree 45 meters (150 feet) high.

With the helicopter thundering above the platform, the three Americans were lowered one at a time in a basket. By the time Elizalde joined them, they were already beginning to feel seasick from the platform's dipping and swaying. Their gear followed in a small cargo net, and as it hit the platform a camera bag spilled out and began to skid. Before anyone could grab it, it slid right over the platform's edge and plunged, disappearing through the green leaf cover.

It seemed like forever before they finally heard the tiny tinkle of its crash on the forest floor below.

Fortunately there was no wind—though later crews would report white-knuckling descents down a rope ladder that swung wildly in high winds.

Below the jungle's leafy canopy the brilliant sunlight was replaced by an eery, soft green gloom. At the bottom of the ladder a Tboli guide dressed only in a loincloth stood waiting. Elizalde climbed down first, easily and quickly. As the Americans followed, the branches of nearby trees caught on their packs and clothes, so they had to move slowly, placing their hands and feet very carefully. When everyone had regrouped and shouldered their gear, the guide waved at them all to follow.

For an hour or more the party padded along a faint trail, climbing and ducking through tangles of rattan, bamboo, and vines. The jungle was dark and humid. Occasional shafts of sunlight stabbed downward whenever the trees above them shifted their crowns. Everyone but the Tboli guide found it hard to keep his footing on the slippery ground. The Americans stumbled often over ankle-high roots.

But what they found when they reached the Tasaday caves was even more wonderful than they'd been led to expect.

The Tasaday caves were rugged and dusty, but the Tasaday lived there quite happily. They greeted everyone with hugs and sniff-kisses—especially Elizalde, who handed out small packets of cookies and salt. Once the greetings were over, the Tasaday cleared a space around the fire and invited their visitors to join them in a special feast of live tadpoles and grubs dipped in palm pith.

Over the next several days, the journalists found themselves increasingly charmed and impressed by their Stone Age hosts. The Tasaday lived the kind of life that most people around the world could only dream of—a life of complete peace, contentment, and harmony. They didn't have words in their language for "weapons," "enemies," or "war." Everybody seemed to get along with everybody else. Younger children were constantly being patted, nuzzled, and praised. Men and women lived as equals, with no class structure—the Tasaday didn't even seem to have a leader. Everyone's opinions and suggestions around the campfire were treated with equal respect. There was always much singing and laughter, with children fearlessly swinging on long vines and scurrying up and down tree trunks with amazing agility.

National Geographic rushed its first photo article about the Tasaday into print several months later ("First Glimpse of a Stone Age Tribe"). CBS broadcast a follow-up *National Geographic* documentary ("The Last Tribes of the Mindanao") in January of 1972. Being two of the largest and most reputable media outlets, their stories reached a huge audience.

People the world over fell in love with the Tasaday. They adored the photographs of naked Tasaday cave mothers nursing and cuddling their babies, and wide-eyed Tasaday children gazing at the camera with cute bewilderment. The documentary proved to be one of the society's all-time greatest hits. "The Tasaday have given the world a new measure for man," enthused one of its editors. "If our ancient ancestors were like the Tasaday, we come of far better stock than I thought."

Other journalists Elizalde took to meet the Tasaday had similar experiences. The Tasaday, they reported, had learned how to live their lives in an almost perfect balance. By working together as a group they were able to reduce the boredom of food-gathering to a few hours a day; the rest were spent singing, telling stories, just goofing around, or sleeping. The children grew up without stress or pressure, and were well behaved. They were also very comfortable around adults, and didn't separate themselves off into groups or cliques.

Anthropologists were fascinated (and also puzzled) to discover that, unlike most other primitive peoples, the Tasaday seemed to feel no need to create cave paintings or make musical instruments. Instead of making pottery or mats or cloth—although there was plenty of raw material around—they just ate and drank out of their cupped hands, boiled water in hollowed-out bamboo sticks, and covered their genitals with leaves kept in place by vines.

Another thing that was curious was that the Tasaday brewed no alcoholic drinks, and didn't smoke or chew tobacco. This was *really* unusual. Anthropologists had never encountered a people who didn't practice at least one of those habits.

Then there was the matter of religious traditions. The Tasaday didn't seem to have any. They married, but didn't perform big marriage celebrations. Each man took only one wife (though they indicated they wouldn't mind having more wives if more became available). When people died, they were simply buried in shallow unmarked graves without ceremony. When asked if they believed in an afterlife, a heaven, or a hell, the Tasaday looked confused. The questions didn't make any sense to them.

They also worshipped no gods or prophets—although their

ancestors *had* promised them that someday, if they stayed patiently in their forest, a Good Person would come to them, bringing much joy and good fortune. That person, the Tasaday had decided, was Manuel Elizalde Jr., whom they called "Momo Bong" (Divine Being), and it was this belief that always gave his visits a special meaning for them. It also explained why they didn't seem to want to have any direct contact with outsiders, even after they'd become aware that other native tribes—the Tboli and the Blit—lived only a few days' walk through the jungle from their caves. In any dealings with non-Tasadays, they always chose Elizalde as their spokesman and go-between.

As the stories and reports multiplied, so did calls for greater protection for the Tasaday against the advancing logging and mining companies. When Elizalde launched his Tasaday Preservation Fund, many prominent western environmentalists and politicians joined him to help raise money. Even the aging Charles Lindbergh, America's most famous pilot, joined the fight. Following a visit to the Tasaday, he pronounced them "the keepers of an ancient wisdom that modern man has almost forgotten."

When President Marcos announced a year later that he was setting aside a 19,000-hectare (47,000-acre) section of the Tasaday jungle as a protected native reserve, he was cheered and applauded around the world.

For three years a steady stream of journalists and scientists visited the Tasaday—but always for only a few hours at a time, and always accompanied by Elizalde. Then, in 1974, Elizalde abruptly cancelled all further access to them. He said he was afraid they might accidentally catch modern diseases like smallpox, tuberculosis, or polio. He also claimed that the Tasadays were finding the interviews too exhausting, and that their lives were becoming distorted by too much contact with modern people.

But by then a virtual "Tasaday industry" had developed, and was flourishing in schools and universities all over the world. In 1975 the first full-length Tasaday book appeared, entitled *The Gentle Tasaday: A Stone Age People in the Philippine Rain Forest,* by the American journalist John Nance. Other books, and hundreds of reports and scientific papers, followed.

Scholars and scientists studying the Tasaday began to question many of the assumptions they had made about how people in the Stone Age used to live. Maybe, for example, our ancestors weren't necessarily as aggressive and warlike as we assumed. Maybe our popular image of Stone Age man as a hairy hulk with ape-like arms, whose method of proposing marriage was to grab his chosen woman by the hair and drag her into his cave—maybe this was all nonsense.

Many conferences and seminars were held, and some scholars began to revise the books and textbooks they'd written about the Stone Age. The well-spoken and Harvard-educated Elizalde became a popular speaker on the academic lecture circuit. Even the world-famous Smithsonian Institute invited him to Washington to speak about the Tasaday.

During all this time, a few renegade journalists and academics had steadfastly refused to go along with the excitement.

These protesters—many of them people who had been refused access to the Tasaday—simply didn't trust Elizalde, or any project he was associated with. They felt he was just using the Tasaday to get a lot of media attention for himself. They accused him of playing the role of "big daddy" to the Philippine aboriginal community.

And anyway, what was he doing with the millions of dollars that were being donated by western media corporations and environmentalists to his Tasaday Preservation Fund?

Others challenged the very idea that the Tasaday were Stone Age people. They asked how a tribe of so few people could have survived so long without obvious signs of inbreeding.

A dietitian wondered how the Tasaday were even managing to stay alive on a daily calorie intake that was lower than the generally accepted level for basic survival.

A Filipino linguist felt the Tasaday language was too similar to the dialects of the region's Tboli and Manobo tribes to have remained isolated for thousands of years. He even claimed he'd overheard two Tasaday men in private conversation using words that sounded oddly like "cement," "house roof," and "pickup truck"!

And why had Elizalde kept all the interviews with the Tasaday so short? Why had he monitored them so carefully, and even tried to control what scientists had written about the Tasaday?

Elizalde dismissed all these objections as sour grapes. They were simply the complaints of grumblers who were jealous of his and the Tasaday's worldwide popularity. If they couldn't live with that, it was their problem.

The world's love affair with the Tasaday continued.

By the early 1980s the location of the Tasaday was no longer much of a secret, but Elizalde's army continued to provide an effective defense against all unauthorized entry into their territory. But when Philippine Opposition Leader Benigno Aquino was murdered in 1983, and the Marcos government was suspected of being involved, Marcos's regime began to crumble. It wasn't long before Elizalde's army—which had been paid by the Philippine government—began to crumble too.

A Swiss journalist by the name of Oswald Iten was one of the first to hear these political rumors in early 1986. Known as a radical, Iten loved to tangle with governments and their institutions. He had already been jailed several times for going into countries where he wasn't welcome. Sensing a scoop, he caught a flight to Davao airport, where he linked up with a local journalist named Joey Lozano. Lozano knew how to get to the Tasaday caves.

The two men managed to make their way through the rainforest to the edge of the Mindanaoan jungle—becoming the first people to manage an unauthorized entry into the Tasaday reserve.

When they arrived at the caves, however, they were startled by what they found.

The caves were empty.

The Tasaday had disappeared.

This was a puzzle. It was widely said that the Tasaday never strayed far from their caves. The two men looked around and then began investigating in earnest.

Their second discovery was that, despite supposedly having lived in these caves since the Stone Age, the Tasaday appeared to have produced very little evidence of ever having lived there. No old or broken tools lying around. No garbage. No forgotten or abandoned personal possessions.

Their third discovery was a trail, camouflaged near the caves but well defined farther along. It led toward the village of Blit at the jungle's edge.

In Blit, the journalists were in for an even bigger surprise. They were told that the Tasaday often came out of the jungle to visit the village—and that they often ate at the village's foodstalls. "Manda [Elizalde] gives them money," a Blit native told Iten.

"There are no Tasaday anyway," another scoffed. "That's just an invented name. It means mountain or something."

But Iten's biggest discovery came several days later when the two reporters finally found the last piece of the puzzle.

They found many of the alleged Stone-Agers living in a scattering of frame huts just inside the jungle. They were wearing Harley-Davidson T-shirts, Nike sneakers, and Levi jeans.

They were also wearing watches and smoking cigarettes.

The Tasaday, it turned out, were nothing more than local natives who had been convinced by Elizalde to pose as prehistoric cave dwellers. "Manda told us if we went naked and were nice to the foreigners, we'd get money because we looked poor," one of them explained. "We only went to the caves when Manda brought in the foreigners. When they flew away, we went back home."

Oswald Iten hurried home and gave the story to the Swiss newspaper *Neue Zuricher Zeitung.* Its three-page story on April 12, 1986 was headlined "Steinzeitschwindel!" (Stone Age Scam!). Two days later the Reuters news agency picked up the story and sent it around the world.

British and American television crews, including journalists from ABC's investigative program *20/20,* quickly followed Iten's trail. They confirmed the whole bizarre story.

Manuel Elizalde Jr., it appeared, had cooked up the Tasaday scam largely as a fund-raising device to fatten up the bank accounts of his Ministry for National Minorities. For a while, as the first millions poured into the Tasaday Preservation Fund, he had even used some of the funds to benefit the natives under his care, providing food and military protection against the local militias and outlaw logging companies who were threatening to overrun them from all sides.

But once Ferdinand Marcos's government began to fall apart and Elizalde realized that he would probably be exposed, he forgot all about his promises. He couldn't face the humiliation, the likelihood of years in jail, or the poverty. Maybe Elizalde really had cared about the native people of the Philippines at one time, but now he cared about himself a lot more.

And so, late in 1983, Manuel Elizalde Jr. had helped himself to the money in his ministry's bank accounts and the Tasaday Preservation Fund—variously estimated at 150 to 250 million dollars—and bought himself an airline ticket to Costa Rica. Costa Rica had no extradition treaty with the Republic of the Philippines, so the Philippines police wouldn't be able to bring him back.

World media reaction to Elizalde's caper was predictably selective. Most of the large newspaper or television corporations that had been fooled by Elizalde were too embarassed to give the story front-page coverage. Many of them gave it no coverage at all. Their smaller, poorer competitors, on the other hand, were happy to give the story lots of attention, and to point out how thoroughly the large corporations had been scammed.

It was much the same within the academic community. Those scientists who had been most deeply involved and whose reputations were most at risk generally worked hardest at damage control. And in 1988, the American Anthropological Society used its annual general meeting to host a special inquiry into "The Tasaday Controversy." Its members split hairs, argued over definitions and spouted jargon until the issue had become so impenetrable, they couldn't decide one way or the other. So they did what they always did when they couldn't agree: called for more study and set up another committee.

Manuel Elizalde Jr. was never brought to justice—but maybe justice found him anyway. After living the high life in Costa Rica for about ten years, Elizalde reportedly became addicted to crack cocaine and ended up squandering his fortune.

He died penniless in 1997—even poorer than the "Tasaday" natives he had used so effectively to con the world.

The Great Shakespeare Forgery

WILLIAM HENRY IRELAND was 16 years old and really depressed.

It was 1793 and he had recently been kicked out of school in London, England, for being (in the words of his principal) "incorrigibly stupid." He was supposed to be studying law, but he hated the subject—he had a passion for books and writing poetry.

To make matters worse, his father, Samuel Ireland, had agreed with the principal. He'd spent a lot of money keeping William in school, hoping his son would bring the family some class by becoming a rich lawyer. But William just wouldn't cooperate.

Being kicked out of school was the last straw. Samuel Ireland decided to forget about further schooling for William, and apprenticed him to a local lawyer as a lowly clerk.

For William, that really hurt. Not just the boring job, sitting all boring day in a dusty cubbyhole filing boring law documents— no, it was his father's cruel putdown as well. For reasons William just couldn't understand, his father had always treated him like a hopeless dolt. And this despite the fact that William really admired his father, and always tried his best to please him.

There were two sore points between William and his father, and one of them always made William despair because there wasn't a thing he could do about it. Often when his parents were fighting, his father hinted that his mother had been unfaithful and that William wasn't really his son. William didn't think this was true—his mother denied it—but his father was obviously not convinced. He seemed to feel that as a result of this public shame, his own career as a bookseller with a shop that barely paid the bills was somehow William's fault.

The other point was William's poetry. You would have thought that a man who sold books and absolutely adored William Shakespeare (Samuel called him "The Immortal Bard") would appreciate a son who wrote poetry. But once again, no luck. Samuel had looked at William's verses once or twice, but had tossed them aside. "Real poetry requires genius," he'd said. "Real genius. Now Shakespeare—there's true genius!"

Samuel Ireland was so obsessed with William Shakespeare that he made his family listen to readings from Shakespeare's plays and poems every single evening after dinner. He'd even made a pilgrimage to Stratford-on-Avon, Shakespeare's birthplace, where he'd bought a chair and a purse that were supposed to have belonged to Shakespeare.

William was pretty sure they were just stupid fakes.

Like many literary men of his time, Samuel Ireland was puzzled about why so little was known about Shakespeare's life, and why hardly any documents featuring his signature or handwriting had ever been found. It was one of the big mysteries surrounding William Shakespeare. How could a man become so famous yet leave behind so little proof of his everyday life? There were even some scholars who explained this by claiming that Shakespeare had never existed at all—that his plays had been written by some-one who'd just used "William Shakespeare" as a pen name.

Samuel Ireland thought that was rubbish. He was sure there was a more logical explanation. He suspected that someone had simply collected all of Shakespeare's papers long before the rest of the world realized how valuable they would become, and was now waiting for the right moment to cash in. "I'd give my entire book collection for just one signature of The Immortal Bard!" he kept telling anyone who would listen.

He said it so often that it eventually put an idea into William's head.

What if he could make his father's dream come true?

At work, William handled a lot of old documents—land deeds, mortgage certificates, and court records. He could also get his hands on some aged parchment—the endpapers in old lawbooks, or empty pages in old court documents.

It wasn't hard to imagine how much happier his relationship with his father might become if he could put these materials to some inspired use.

William borrowed a copy of *Steven's Shakespeare,* a collection of Shakespeare's works that contained a printed version of William Shakespeare's signature. On an afternoon when he was alone in the office—fortunately, his office wasn't very busy and he was often alone—he studied the signature carefully.

Hmm. That didn't look so hard.

He practiced the signature again and again, until he'd filled several pages with it. It wasn't long before it began to look quite convincing.

William took a deep breath and decided to go for it.

He consulted a printer's apprentice on what to mix into ordinary ink to make it look more aged. He rummaged around and found a 17th-century land title deed to use as a model. Then he slowly, carefully wrote out a deed for some land near London's Globe Theatre, where Shakespeare's plays had been performed. He listed Shakespeare as the buyer and a Michael Fraser as the seller. He signed Shakespeare's name with his right hand, Fraser's with his left, then pressed a wax seal on the parchment.

Of course, he still needed a good story to make his "discovery" believable. For this, he invented a "Mr. H." He told his father that Mr. H. was a client for whom he'd managed to find a long-lost, very important legal document. In gratitude, the man had allowed him to dig through an old chest full of ancient papers in his attic and take anything he wanted. Mr. H.'s only condition had been to make William swear never to reveal his real name.

Just as William had hoped, Samuel Ireland was ecstatic—especially after he'd shown the document to another bookseller who'd pronounced it genuine. Suddenly, he looked at his son with new eyes. Maybe he had underestimated the boy. Here was evidence of both intelligence and enterprise! What an inspired idea it had been to apprentice him to a lawyer.

And this Mr. H. had a whole chestful of ancient documents in his attic?

"Yes, father." William could already hear the next question coming, but he was so pleased with his father's response that he didn't care.

"And might there be other documents involving Shakespeare in that chest? Documents that could throw even more light on the life of The Immortal Bard?"

His father's delight was making William feel giddy and reckless. Yes, he agreed, there might be other documents. He'd have another look at the earliest possible opportunity.

And so, during the following two years, William kept "finding" more and more documents of the sort his father prized.

A letter addressed to William Shakespeare relating to the land deed.

A receipt from the actor John Heminge for money received from William Shakespeare.

Then an entire letter in Shakespeare's own handwriting to the Earl of Southampton, thanking him for his support and patronage.

Finally—because William had often heard his Protestant father worry that Shakespeare might have been a Catholic, and Samuel hated Catholics—he found a "Confession of Faith" in Shakespeare's own handwriting, apparently written shortly before his death, confirming his allegiance to the Protestant Church of England.

Samuel Ireland thought this was marvelous, splendid—magnificent beyond belief. After receiving Shakespeare's "Confession of Faith," he even sent invitations to a number of famous writers and scholars, offering them the chance to examine his treasures for themselves. These included the biographer James Boswell, the scholar and clergyman Reverend Samuel Parr, and England's poet laureate Henry James Pye.

To the Irelands' delight, they all accepted. As they trooped into his family's modest home, William could clearly see that his family's status was rising. Everyone expressed their congratulations in the most glowing terms. When Samuel brought out the documents, there was a breathless silence. Each man examined the bundle in turn.

It took them only a short time to pronounce everything authentic. In fact, James Boswell was so moved by Shakespeare's "Confession of Faith" that he knelt and actually kissed the parchment, saying, "Thank God I have lived to see this page!"

William never forgot that night—that amazing night when three of England's most famous scholars and writers sat right there in his own living room, praising his work without even realizing it.

Yes, he'd always known he wasn't "incorrigibly stupid"—but maybe he was actually discovering that the very opposite was true! After all, people said that Shakespeare hadn't been a particularly first-rate student—and Shakespeare hadn't even been studying law.

Was the opposite of "incorrigibly stupid" something like "real genius"?

William decided to test his theory a little more.

He told his father that Mr. H. had given him permission to search beyond the old chest in his attic. He was now allowed to explore his entire house.

And sure enough, over the next half year a whole new bonanza of Shakespearean treasures appeared. A love poem from Shakespeare to his future wife, Anne Hathaway. Some books from Shakespeare's personal library, with his handwritten notations in the margins. Then a startling discovery: a letter to Shakespeare from Queen Elizabeth I herself, expressing her appreciation of his literary achievements.

Samuel Ireland was almost beside himself with glee. This was exactly as he'd predicted! Hadn't he said that sooner or later the Bard's papers would appear?

William laughed happily. Life could be very good.

Mind you, life could also be tricky. At work, William was having more and more trouble keeping his growing forging operation under wraps. At first, before he'd known much about how to do it, he'd worked with a single bottle of doctored ink and any old kind of parchment. He'd learned a lot since then. By now, when he really got going, the place looked like a chemistry lab. Bottles of inks, acids, emulsifiers, and watercolors; paintbrushes, boxfuls of pens, and dozens of nibs; many different kinds of paper and parchment; candles, sealing wax, ribbons, and erasing rubber.

Fortunately, his employer rarely came in before noon, but there had been a few scary moments.

Once another clerk from a nearby law office had barged in unexpectedly and William had had to scramble desperately to explain his activities—he'd told the boy he was just "restoring" an old collection of poetry.

But his friend Robert Talbot, who had dropped by one day without warning, hadn't believed the explanation. "What are you *really* doing, William?" he had grinned. William had eventually had to confess and swear Robert to secrecy.

Samuel Ireland now made William a startling proposal. He felt that these magnificent treasures had to be shared with the entire world. The Irelands couldn't just keep them selfishly for themselves. So he proposed they publish the entire collection under the title *Miscellaneous Papers and Legal Instruments under the Hand and Seal of William Shakespeare.* In the meantime, he would display the collection with great fanfare in his bookshop. Was William agreeable to that?

William certainly was.

Both the news and the collection attracted instant public attention. A steady stream of customers, both scholars and ordinary folk, came around to examine William's extraordinary finds. The shop was full from morning till night. Even the Prince of Wales stopped by to have a look. Samuel couldn't stop talking about it for days.

Filled with a growing confidence, and lulled by the fact that nobody was challenging his forgeries, William now decided to tackle the plays themselves. Early in 1795, once his father had published the *Miscellaneous Papers,* William announced that he had found the original manuscripts of *King Lear* and parts of *Hamlet*—written in Shakespeare's own handwriting!

This was really upping the ante. A letter, a poem, or a deed was one thing. The plays themselves were quite another. To Samuel, this was almost like finding parts of the original Bible. As he held the parchments reverently in his hands, Samuel wondered aloud whether William could truly appreciate how precious this manuscript was.

From the look on his father's face, William had no trouble imagining it. He realized that he loved being able to give this happiness to his father. He also realized that for the first time in his life he didn't feel like a child anymore.

The excitement increased even further when scholars examining the manuscripts found them to be significantly different from existing published versions. (Since his father had always frowned at the racier parts in these plays, William had "improved" them by removing anything sexy and writing his own patches to fill the holes.) Once again the delighted Samuel Ireland lavished praise on his son and promised to publish his discoveries for the benefit of Shakespeare lovers everywhere.

It was at this point that the first public doubts began to surface. Writing in the London *Morning Herald,* Shakespeare expert J.A. Boaden regretted to say that after examining the Shakespeare documents in Mr. Ireland's shop, he felt they were probably forgeries. He said he'd had his doubts from the start, but hadn't wanted to say anything until he'd made a thorough study of the matter. With all due respect to his colleagues, he felt they were letting themselves get swept away by the excitement. Other correspondents agreed. Questions about the mysterious Mr. H. increased.

Then the drama critic Edmond Malone weighed in with a list of puzzling errors and inconsistencies in the documents, including the signature of the actor John Heminge, which he claimed differed considerably from other authenticated examples. Pressure mounted on the Irelands to reveal the true source of all these papers.

But the Irelands had their defenders too. Reverend Samuel Parr rallied a large group of influential supporters—enough to fill an entire page with signatures—who issued a joint statement insisting that Boaden and Malone were quite wrong, and that the documents were definitely genuine.

The debate quickly became more heated and widespread—especially in the newspapers. "Shakespeare Documents Suspect" read one headline. "Bookseller Doubted" claimed another. "Shakespeare Mystery Man Sought" announced a third.

Samuel Ireland pronounced it all rubbish. "Of course these documents are genuine," he insisted. "Some of the most knowledgeable scholars in England have said so."

We can only wonder exactly what provoked William Ireland to do what he did next. Obviously his self-confidence had grown to the point where he really did feel his writing and forging abilities had improved enough to get away with it. Maybe he thought he could silence his doubters if he produced the biggest, most astonishing find of all—a brand-new, never before seen or heard of Shakespearean play. In fact, not just one, but *two* of them!

That's what he told his father soon after his *Lear* and *Hamlet* versions had been published. He said he'd found the manuscripts of two unknown plays entitled *Vortigern and Rowena* and *Henry II,* both in Shakespeare's own style and handwriting. But this time there was a catch. Mr. H. was not willing to let these plays out of his hands, and so had only agreed to let William copy them out by hand.

The news of this discovery stunned Samuel Ireland. For a man who worshipped William Shakespeare, this was almost too much to handle. The discovery of two new plays would put

Shakespeare lovers everywhere into an uproar. This would make father and son famous all over the world!

He urged William to make those copies as fast as he possibly could.

William was already doing that. He had found the story of *Vortigern and Rowena* in Raphael Holinshed's *Chronicles of England, Scotland and Ireland*—the same history book that Shakespeare had often used for his plots. Vortigern was an Anglo-Saxon king who had murdered his way to the top—not unlike Shakespeare's *Macbeth*. For the next four months William slaved away over this story, turning it into a five-act imitation Shakespeare play.

By February of 1796 he was able to show his father the results.

For Samuel Ireland, any work by The Immortal Bard was brilliant, was magnificent—and so, of course, was this.

"Really?" William wanted to know.

A work of unquestionable genius, his father declared firmly. Absolutely.

William let out the breath he'd been holding without realizing it. He had to turn away to keep his relief and pride from showing. Finally—an original work of "real genius"!

But Richard Sheridan, owner of the Drury Lane Theatre, to whom Samuel showed the play, wasn't so sure. "There are certainly some bold ideas here," he agreed. "But they're rather crude and undigested. Shakespeare must have been very young when he wrote this play."

Nevertheless, Sheridan offered to produce the work in his theater in April of that year. He proposed to split the proceeds between himself and the Irelands, half and half.

News of the discovery and upcoming production of *Vortigern and Rowena* spread across England like wildfire. Once mostly of interest to scholars and theater-lovers, the issue now became a national hot topic. People talked about it in England's pubs and taverns. It was the dominant subject at parties and public gatherings. It was discussed at the universities and colleges. Even the king was rumored to be interested.

April 2, 1796 was definitely shaping up to be one of the most controversial premieres in the history of the English theater.

While the debate in the newspapers and tabloids seemed willing to give the Irelands the benefit of the doubt, it was a different story at the Drury Lane Theatre. "I know you don't think much of it, but we're going to put it on anyway," Sheridan told his stage manager, John Kemble, firmly. "Do the best you can."

Kemble pulled a face. He didn't just dislike the play, he hated it. He was convinced it was bogus, and so were many of his actors. Some of them even refused to accept parts in the production.

When the play opened on April 2, the open-air theater was bursting with people. Every nook and cranny in the building was crammed. There were people sitting on the roof, and even in the branches of some nearby trees. William and his father, who were seated in one of the boxes, received repeated cheers from the crowd.

But only minutes after the curtain rose, everything began to fall apart. It quickly became clear that no one in the production was taking the play seriously. The actors hammed it up, bumbling around the stage, mixing up their lines and cracking jokes. They seemed intent on sabotaging the whole performance.

Soon a growing part of the audience was laughing along with the actors, to the annoyance of those who still believed in the play. There were jeers and catcalls. People threw hats and gloves onto the stage. Then they started throwing them at each other.

Arguments erupted. Fights broke out. When the final curtain fell, the theater was a shambles.

The Irelands hurriedly ducked out a side door and hid in an alley until the crowd had dispersed. They were both badly shaken.

Sheridan later announced that all further performances of *Vortigern and Rowena* were cancelled. It had been the worst audience reaction to any play he'd produced in the entire 25 years of his theatrical career.

After the disaster at the Drury Lane Theatre, public opinion turned against the Irelands. Fewer and fewer people now believed in the authenticity of the Shakespeare documents.

Most suspected that the Irelands had been duped, but a growing number began to accuse Samuel Ireland of having committed the fraud himself. In public, Samuel defended himself vigorously, but in private he asked William more and more desperately to reveal Mr. H.'s identity, or at least arrange a meeting with him so all this confusion could be straightened out.

William was being driven deeper and deeper into a corner. Finally, he couldn't think of any other way to end this disaster but to confess the whole mess to his father.

So he did that. He told his father what he had done. He apologized. He said he had never intended for any of this to happen.

At first Samuel Ireland looked confused. He asked William what he was going on about.

William tried to explain that he'd gotten carried away when he'd seen how happy all his discoveries were making his father.

Samuel's forehead remained creased in puzzlement. Then his face softened. He assured William that this wasn't necessary. It was appreciated, certainly, but it wouldn't solve anything. The solution was for Samuel to meet Mr. H. and for the two men to sort things out. That was the solution.

Now it was William's turn to be puzzled. "But there is no Mr. H., Father. I just told you—I forged them all."

His father was becoming impatient. He told William to stop this foolishness—it would never work. Did he really think that anyone would believe that a mere boy could have written anything by The Immortal Bard?

William became alarmed. "But it's true, Father! I can prove it." He stopped and then looked directly at his father. "You *know* I fabricated those documents, don't you? Those documents, and the play?"

Samuel had had enough of this. He was sure William meant well, but now he was giving himself airs. It was unseemly. As William abruptly turned and fled from the room, Samuel yelled after him: "For heaven's sake, boy, you couldn't even pass your examinations at school!"

It was the last time father and son spoke to each other.

The next day William sent his father a letter describing in great detail how he had gone about producing his scams—even including some of his drafts and discards.

His father barely glanced at them. He called it all a pack of rubbish.

William tried to use his brother and sister, who both believed him, as go-betweens. It only made their father angrier. He called William a vain and selfish ignoramus.

William packed a suitcase and left the family home for good.

During the following year, living in a basement room and still working in the office, he wrote and published a pamphlet entitled *An Authentic Account of the Shaksperian Manuscripts.* It contained a full and detailed confession, with evidence and apologies, including a full exoneration of his father.

Samuel Ireland published an angry denial and disinherited his son.

Unfortunately for William, the public sided with his father. No one seemed willing to accept that William was intelligent enough to have fooled so many scholars. They all blamed Samuel—who went to his grave four years later discredited and disgraced, still insisting the documents were genuine.

For a while, William kept trying to set things straight. In 1805 he published an entire book on the subject, entitled *The Confessions of William Ireland*. The book didn't sell many copies. Eventually he gave up trying and began writing novels instead—over a dozen under various pseudonyms—to give himself a fresh start. They were reasonably successful, but they weren't works of genius.

Ironically, William's most successful publication became a complete catalog of Shakespeare's works—which didn't include *Vortigern and Rowena* and *Henry II*.

War of the Worlds:
A Martian Invasion

ON THE EVENING OF SUNDAY, October 30, 1938, people in the United States tuning in to their local CBS radio station around 8:15 p.m. heard an electrifying news bulletin.

"We interrupt this program for a special bulletin from Trenton, New Jersey," an excited-sounding announcer exclaimed. "At 7:50 p.m. a huge, flaming object, believed to be a meteorite, fell on a farm in the neighborhood of Grovers Mill, New Jersey, 22 miles from Trenton. The flash in the sky was visible within a radius of several hundred miles, and the noise of the impact was heard as far north as Elizabeth!"

He informed the audience that CBS had dispatched a special mobile unit to the scene, and that CBS commentator Carl Phillips would give a live description of the event as soon as he could reach the site from his present location in Princeton.

Within moments, Phillips reported in from Wilmuth Farm. He had to shout to make himself heard over a background of crackling and hissing sounds. He described a sight that was eerie and unsettling. The object didn't look much like a meteor—not really, no. It appeared to be an enormous cylinder, about 30 meters (100 feet) in diameter. The cylinder lay partly buried now, in a huge crater, and was sheathed in a strange-looking, yellowish-white metal—maybe some sort of extraterrestrial material...

His voice was briefly drowned out by a burst of static, then rose to overcome the sound of police sirens. A growing crowd of

34

spectators was now pushing in toward the pit, he reported—despite police efforts to hold them back. Some of the people had driven their cars right up to the crater. Their headlights were shining like spotlights on the half-buried object.

Then a strange humming began to rise out of the pit. Could his radio listeners hear it? Phillips moved his microphone closer. There. Could they hear it now? A deep buzzing sound drifted up through radio speakers, as well as faint shouts and commands: "Keep back! Keep back!!"

Suddenly Phillips's voice rose sharply. The top of the cylinder was beginning to turn! It was rotating—like a screw top! It appeared to be hollow inside. Someone yelled for people to watch out, that thing was red hot; people were going to get burned! Then there was the clank of a large piece of metal falling to the ground, hitting something hard.

Phillips's voice was now shaking with excitement. Something had begun crawling out of the opened cylinder! Something with two huge luminous disks... were they eyes?...a face? No, it looked like the head of a kind of huge snake, its skin like wet leather...wriggling out...tentacles...a second head, and then a third! Their mouths were V-shaped, with saliva dripping from them...too horrible to look at! People were stumbling back, running...

Now another shape was rising out of the pit, Phillips reported. A humped, mechanical-looking thing, on metal legs...or metal supports of some kind. Phillips didn't know what to make of it. Suddenly a brilliant ray of light shot out, bouncing against a kind of mirror—a mirror aimed at the crowd. But no, this wasn't just light, it was... it was flame, a huge jet of flame blasting straight at the crowd, turning them all into flaming torches, a solid mass of flame!

Radio speakers vibrated with the screams of agonized people. Sounds of explosions. Phillips shouted that everything was on fire, everything! The forest, the farm buildings, the cars—it was spreading fast! And it was coming his way! There were more screams, yells, another crash, another stunningly loud explosion that could have blown the cloth out of a radio speaker. Then, abruptly, crackling dead air…

After a few seconds, the station returned. An announcer apologized for the interruption. He regretted to report that CBS had just received word that at least 40 people had been burned to death in a field east of Grovers Mill. One of the bodies was that of CBS reporter Carl Phillips. Four companies of state troopers were being brought in from Trenton to commence military operations, and to help residents of the area evacuate their homes.

The reporter then announced that CBS had received a request from the Trenton militia to make its network available to the military for further communications with the American public. In view of the seriousness of the situation, CBS had agreed, and was handing over its broadcast facilities to Militia Field Headquarters, where a Captain Lansing was standing by.

There was a clatter of microphone sounds, and then a clipped, confident voice identified itself as Captain Lansing of the state militia signal corps, in the vicinity of Grovers Mill. Lansing assured the American public that the situation arising from the appearance of certain creatures of unknown origin on the Wilmuth farm was totally under control. Whatever was in that pit was now completely surrounded, he said. Eight battalions of infantry armed with rifles and machine guns stood ready to blast it to smithereens.

He sounded almost condescending. Whatever they were, these creatures wouldn't dare raise their heads out of the pit again. No, sir, not with searchlights and hundreds of machine guns focused on them at close range all around the pit's rim. No, this wouldn't take much time at all, Lansing said, and it was a good chance for the troops to get a little target practice.

There was a pause, and then a note of uncertainty crept into his voice. He was seeing something rising out of the cylinder. Just a shadow, perhaps? No, it was moving, all right. Hard to make out... a shield-like thing, rising higher and higher above the cylinder. Looked like solid metal, whatever it was. It was still rising! Now it was higher than the surrounding trees! Lansing's voice had lost its professional cool. What was going on? This thing was standing up... rearing up on metal legs... "*Hold on there!*"

There was a rush of air and a thunderous blast that sounded like gasoline exploding. Then the radio transmission went dead again.

When the broadcast resumed, an announcer from New York had replaced the one in Trenton. It was obvious that this man could barely suppress his panic. In a special news bulletin, he informed the American public that the battle in Grovers Mill had resulted in one of the worst military disasters in modern times. The strange creatures that had emerged from a half-buried cylinder at the Wilmuth farm were part of an invading army from Mars; of the 7,000 fully armed troops that had engaged the enemy, only 120 were known to have survived. Dead bodies littered the fields from Grovers Mill to Plainsboro, either crushed by the invaders' machinery or incinerated by the death ray.

The announcer stopped, trying to get a grip on himself. He was breathing heavily. When he resumed, he said the invaders were now in control of central New Jersey, and that telephone and telegraph lines had been torn down from Pennsylvania to New York. Many railroad tracks had been ripped up; most trains had stopped running. Highways in all directions were jammed with fleeing people. Police and army reserves were trying to restore order, but with little success. Martial law had been declared in New Jersey and eastern Pennsylvania.

There was a brief pause, during which the audience could hear urgent whispers and the faint sound of shortwave radio squawking. "We take you now," the announcer continued hastily, "to Washington, for a special broadcast on this national emergency by the Secretary of the Interior..."

What over 5 million CBS radio listeners were listening to— though a surprisingly large number didn't realize it—was a radio dramatization of *War of the Worlds,* a futuristic novel about a Martian attack on the planet Earth by the British novelist H.G. Wells. The play's producer, Orson Welles (the similar name is pure coincidence) was then only 23 years old but already a famous enough veteran of American theater to have appeared on the cover of *Time* magazine. Welles had teamed up with radio dramatist Howard Koch to adapt the British novel for American radio.

Welles was known for being willing to do almost anything to make his theatrical productions gripping and memorable. He'd found Wells's novel fascinating, but far too old-fashioned and distant. To make the story more realistic, he had first changed the English locations to American ones, then changed the date to a slightly futuristic 1939 and added powerful modern features such as news bulletins, on-the-spot reporters, and realistic sound effects.

The broadcast was being aired live in a CBS studio, by actors standing in front of microphones with their scripts on music stands before them. When not reading their lines, they all helped produce the sound effects—running on the spot to simulate panicking people, shouting together when the script called for screaming crowds, and banging various objects to produce the other sounds the play required.

Welles stood in the glass-fronted sound booth with his ear-phones on, cueing the actors as their lines came up. Tall and already quite stocky, he looked like a conductor directing a military band. The studio was a busy clutter of microphone cords, music stands, junction boards, and boxfuls of the strange and unlikely gadgets used for radio sound effects: pots, glass jars, hammers, kitchen cutlery, chunks of wood, bags of cornmeal, and a creaky-hinged miniature door in a door frame.

During rehearsals, Welles and his CBS bosses had waged a constant tug-of-war about the play's "realism." The CBS officials believed the play was becoming too realistic, and therefore likely to frighten listeners. That sounded good to both Welles and Koch—in fact, they wanted to increase the realism even more! For example, with audiences already on edge since American radio stations had begun interrupting regular programming with flash news bulletins from Europe (where World War II was about to break out), Welles had nevertheless decided to use that same kind of flash news bulletin in his production. CBS officials had objected, but Welles had refused to budge.

Even so, on the day of the broadcast, Howard Koch had still complained that the play sounded too unlikely. "Nobody's really going to buy this story," he insisted. "It's just too fantastical to believe."

By 8:30 p.m.—half an hour into the broadcast—it was quickly becoming clear just how wrong he was!

The phones began ringing in police stations all over the American northeast around 8:15 p.m.

By 8:20 p.m. people began pouring into the streets, many with wet cloths and towels held over their faces. Sirens wailed, and ambulances jammed emergency entrances at hospitals with people suffering from shock, hysteria, and heart attacks. Militia headquarters in Essex and Sussex counties were swamped with calls from national guardsmen. "When should we report?" they shouted into their telephones. "Should we come down right now?!"

In Indianapolis, a woman ran into a church where a service was going on, screaming, "New York is being destroyed by Martians—it's the end of the world! I just heard it on the radio!" Hospitals received hundreds of calls from doctors and nurses offering to volunteer their services. Somebody pulled the emergency elevator bells at the Hotel Montague in Brooklyn, and patrons poured out of the hotel shouting, "The Martians are coming! The Martians are coming!"

At the Dixie Bus Terminal in midtown Manhattan, people jammed the ticket counters. "Gimme a ticket! Where to? Anywhere! North! South! West! Anywhere but east!" Traffic on all the main highways rose sharply, as heavily loaded cars and trucks scrambled to get out of town. By 9:00 p.m. parts of Trenton, Newark, New York, and Atlantic City were gridlocked, with car horns blaring and thousands of police trying desperately to unsnarl the traffic.

The reaction was less intense in the more western parts of the U.S., but there, too, people were unnerved. Chicago's police and its radio stations were deluged with calls. In San Francisco, newspaper switchboards were jammed. Hysteria gripped the campus of Brevard College in North Carolina—some students fainted; others fought for access to telephones to call their parents. Gas stations everywhere did a roaring business as millions of drivers filled their gas tanks in preparation to flee.

All over the United States, people poured into the streets to watch the night sky for signs of the Martian attacks.

As the hysteria gathered momentum, people even began to *see* what they had heard on the radio. Police started receiving reports of actual sightings. "Yeah, I saw them! Spaceships, Martians! Thousands of them! They bombed Mercerville and they're burning Dutch Neck! You guys got to get out here fast!" Firehalls received calls about explosions—houses, streets, entire villages on fire.

More alarming, a lot of people armed themselves and began shooting at anything that looked even vaguely Martian—people, deer, trees, clouds. The mayor of a city in the Midwest called up CBS in New York City, demanding to speak to Orson Welles. "There are mobs in my streets! There are women and children crowding into my churches!" he shouted into the phone. "There's violence, looting, rioting! If this is some crummy joke, I'm coming to New York to give him one helluva punch in the nose!"

Telephone operators on the CBS switchboard tried their best to calm their callers down. "No, of course it's not really happening—it's just a play. Yes, really. No—didn't you hear the announcement at the beginning of the show? Yes, and there were two more during the show. Honestly! No, no, there aren't any Martians. It's just an adaptation of a... it's just an imaginary... it's just a..." No matter how often they repeated them, their assurances didn't seem to have much effect.

At some point a group of New York City policemen entered the CBS building, thinking to stop the broadcast, but when an officer tried to enter the studio (ignoring the lit-up "ON AIR" sign above the door) an actor, not realizing what was happening out there in the real world, quickly pushed him out and locked the soundproof door.

By the end of the broadcast, the hallways around the studio were crammed with police, reporters, photographers, and gawkers. Finally informed about the situation outside, a delighted Welles and his crew escaped out a back door.

It appeared that his production had been every bit as gripping and memorable as he'd hoped.

The next day, the story of the radio play's effect was headline news in newspapers and radio broadcasts all over the country.

"Nation in Panic from Martian Broadcast," read one headline.

"Not since the Spanish fleet sailed to bombard the New England coast in 1898," the *New York Herald Tribune* stated, "has so much hysteria, panic and sudden conversion to religion been reported to the press."

Many people were indignant at Welles's recklessness. "Radio ought to act promptly to prevent a repetition of the wave of panic in which it inundated the nation," fumed the *New York Times.* Iowa Senator Clyde Herring called Welles a "Hallowe'en bogeyman" who had been more interested in theatrical success than concerned about its potential for damage and distress. He called for a law to curb such performances.

But columnist Dorothy Thompson, in the *New York Herald Tribune,* called it "the story of the century." She felt that the broadcast had demonstrated some hard truths about the American public's gullibility.

"It has shown up the incredible stupidity, lack of nerve and ignorance of thousands," she declared. "It has proved how easy it is to start a mass delusion, [and has] uncovered the primeval fears lying under the thinnest surface of the so-called civilized man." She didn't think Orson Welles ought to be blamed at all. In fact, she suggested he be given a congressional medal or a national prize!

CBS eventually apologized to the public, promising "not to use the technique of a simulated news broadcast within a dramatization when the circumstances could cause immediate alarm to numbers of listeners."

This pledge didn't stop several hundred listeners from suing the network for damages as high as $50,000 for "mental anguish" and "personal injury." However, all of the suits were denied—except for a claim for a pair of black shoes, size 9B, by a man from Massachusetts, who explained that he'd had to spend the money he'd been saving to buy those shoes to escape the invading Martians!

Orson Welles got such a kick out of this claim that he insisted the man be paid—despite the protestations of CBS's lawyers.

But Orson Welles's CBS production of *War of the Worlds* wasn't the only time Howard Koch's adaptation of H.G. Wells's novel was broadcast—and some subsequent productions had remarkably similar effects.

Only six years later, in 1944, a radio station in Santiago, Chile, broadcast the play in Spanish, also using local place names and the names of local politicians.

Once again, despite a disclaimer at the beginning of the show warning listeners that it was just a play, a general panic ensued, with people pouring into the streets and traffic becoming snarled. The governor of one of Chile's provinces telegraphed Chile's Minister of the Interior at government headquarters in Santiago to inform him that provincial troops had been placed on alert and the artillery was ready to repel the Martians by any means at their disposal!

The most serious outcome resulted from a 1949 airing of the play by a radio station in Quito, Ecuador. In this case, the station's artistic director, Leonardo Paez, went so far as to plant fake stories in local newspapers about flying saucers being seen near Quito in the days leading up to his broadcast.

Like his predecessors, Paez also used local place names and the names of real Ecuadorian politicians, but unlike them, he made no announcements alerting his listeners to the fact that the broadcast was a play.

"The town of Latacunga has been destroyed!" a reporter shouted into the microphone. "The air base at Mariscal Sucre has been captured, and thousands have been killed! The Martian invaders are rapidly closing in on Quito! The Minister of the Interior is appealing to Quito's women and children to flee to the mountains, so that the men will be free to defend the city!"

Total hysteria broke out in Quito's streets, as people rushed out to obey the Minister's order.

When the radio producer was told about the panic his broadcast was causing, he stopped the play and appealed to his listeners for calm.

But when Quito's citizens realized they had been deceived, panic turned to fury. A mob gathered in front of the three-story building that housed the radio station. Stones and bricks began to fly. Windows and doors were smashed.

Someone shouted, "Let's set the building on fire!" and several men rushed to the entrance with newspapers and matches.

Within minutes, flames were licking their way up the wooden paneling around the doors. When firefighters arrived, the crowd surged around them, refusing to let them beat down the flames. When the firemen persisted, hooking up their hoses to a nearby fire hydrant, the crowd changed direction and smashed the hydrant. Water gushed out of the broken pipe and flooded the sidewalk. The firemen called the police, but when the police arrived the crowd swarmed the police cars and attacked the officers. One officer was severely beaten and several attackers were shot.

Authorities finally had to call in the army, which used tanks and tear gas to restore order.

The radio station was burned to the ground. In all, six people lost their lives. The actors were arrested and jailed, and Leonardo Paez, afraid for his life, fled the country.

Although Orson Welles (1915–1985) went on to become one of America's most widely known actors, directors, and filmmakers, directing or acting in over 100 plays and films (*Citizen Kane, Moby Dick*), his production of *War of the Worlds* remains his most famous and notorious achievement.

That notoriety has proven so tempting to radio producers that *War of the Worlds* has never stopped being broadcast—despite (or perhaps because of) its tendency to produce panic. Two broadcasts of the play in 1968 (New York and San Antonio) went off without a hitch, but a broadcast on Halloween in 1974 (Providence, Rhode Island) caused considerable disturbance and some lawsuits. A 1981 production in Germany barely raised eyebrows, but a 1988 production by Radio Braga in Portugal provoked such terror among its listeners that over 200 of them stormed the radio station after learning they had been duped.

Orson Welles would have approved. He never regretted the uproar his famous production caused. He said later in his life, about this production as well as others: "Every true artist must, in his own way, be a magician, a charlatan. I have always tried my best to be both."

There's a Sucker Born Every Minute

ON JANUARY 17, 1882, a shocking rumor began to circulate around the city of London, England.

London's Regent Park Zoo, it was said, had sold Jumbo, England's favorite elephant, to a circus in America.

When the park's Zoological Society admitted that the rumor was true, the British public was outraged. The enormous African elephant, at 3.6 meters (12 feet) tall the biggest in the world, had been a fixture at the zoo for more than 20 years. Couples had been photographed beside him for their weddings, and later on with their new babies. Thousands of children had ridden and "grown up" with Jumbo. "Jumbo Sale Provokes Shock, Indignation," the *Daily Telegraph* announced. The zoo was deluged with angry letters and telegrams.

The man to whom Jumbo had been sold—for the astonishing sum of 20,000 pounds (about $50,000)—was the notorious Phineas Taylor Barnum, known in the United States as "The Prince of Humbug." Barnum was the owner of P.T. Barnum's Greatest Show on Earth, a huge circus that toured North America year-round in 48 extra-large railcars. Barnum's plan was to have Jumbo transported to New York by ship. His agent, "Elephant Bill" Newman, had instructions to load Jumbo into a huge wagon-crate and haul him down to the docks for transfer into the waiting freighter, *Assyrian Monarch*.

But Jumbo seemed to have other ideas. Confronted with his

wagon-crate, he would not get in. And when Newman tried to force him in by poking him with a cattle prod, he was so insulted he simply lay down and refused to get up.

No amount of yanking and yelling could change his mind. Newman even tried hauling him up by hitching him to another elephant. It was no use. Jumbo lay stubbornly on his side on the pavement, his massive legs stretched away from his body and his trunk flopping idly about his head.

"Jumbo Doesn't Want to Leave Us!" declared the *Daily Telegraph*. "Jumbo Loyal to the End," announced the *Sunday Times*.

At the news, Londoners swarmed down to Regent Park to witness this amazing act of loyalty. They brought Jumbo peanuts, flowers, and casseroles. A bride brought him a piece of her wedding cake. Someone started a Jumbo Retention Fund, and thousands of children contributed their pennies to buy Jumbo back. The issue was raised and discussed in the British Parliament. Even the queen was said to have made "enquiries."

Alarmed, Elephant Bill Newman telegraphed his boss in New York. PUBLIC OUTCRY ABOUT JUMBO, STOP. UNSURE WHAT TO DO, STOP. AFRAID THIS MAY DELAY OR BLOCK JUMBO SHIPMENT, STOP. PLEASE ADVISE, STOP.

To Newman's surprise, P.T. Barnum replied: NOT WORRIED, STOP. LET HIM LIE THERE FOR A WEEK IF HE WANTS TO, STOP. BEST ADVERTISING IN THE WORLD, STOP. JUST MAKE SURE HE'S WELL FED AND WATERED, STOP.

Newman shouldn't have been surprised, because this was the kind of approach that had already made Barnum famous (and infamous) all over the United States. "A problem is just another word for an opportunity!" he was fond of saying. Another one of his favorite sayings was: "All advertising is good advertising!"

To Barnum, any uproar was a good uproar, and any uproar at

all was worth making bigger. So the famous scam artist devised a clever plan. He secretly sent money to London with instructions to start up a Rescue Jumbo crusade. This group—not realizing they were being financed by the very person they were opposing—used the money to print flyers, take out newspaper advertisements (SAVE OUR JUMBO!), and stage protest rallies (NO, NO, JUMBO WON'T GO!!). The rallies got lots of newspaper coverage.

Very good.

Then Barnum paid for a similar crusade in New York City. This group also printed flyers, took out newspaper advertisements (JUMBO'S OURS NOW—GIVE HIM UP!), and staged protest rallies (WE WANT JUMBO! WE WANT JUMBO!!). These rallies also got lots of newspaper coverage.

Even better.

And once the two organizations became aware of each other, things really heated up. More statements to the press. More letters to the editor. Protest marches. Tremendous uproar!

Beautiful.

But Barnum was only getting started. He now proceeded to fan the flames by paying several British newspaper columnists to urge the public to write protest letters. Soon such letters were pouring into the Office of the British Prime Minister, the Queen's Office at Buckingham Palace, the editorial offices of London's newspapers, and Regent Park's Zoological Society. The Zoological Society received so many, it had to hire extra clerks to answer them all.

The uproar was reaching maximum noise and heat.

When he'd fanned the flames about as high as he thought he could, Barnum began selling Jumbo souvenirs—Jumbo hats, Jumbo neckties, Jumbo frameable prints, Jumbo earrings, bracelets, fans, and trading cards (no T-shirts, because nobody wore T-shirts in those days). There were by now so many upset people coming down to the zoo to visit Jumbo for the last time that they became easy marks for Barnum's aggressive salesmen. The profits started rolling in.

When Jumbo finally decided to get up—almost two weeks later—some columnists wondered whether the event had been rigged, or at least stretched out, by Barnum himself. It probably was. The record isn't entirely clear, but one thing was certain—the journalists were beginning to understand how Barnum operated his scams.

As Jumbo's wagon-crate rolled through London's streets on its way to the docks, tens of thousands of British citizens lined the route to wave goodbye. Of course, since Barnum had organized this event, Jumbo's wagon-crate was being hauled by a dozen splendidly plumed and decorated horses, with a brass band following behind—and since Barnum's salesmen were selling souvenirs all along the way, Jumbo's caravan took an extra-long route to get to the docks.

But even after Jumbo was safely housed in the *Assyrian Monarch*'s forward hold, Barnum didn't let up. Every day, an update on Jumbo's health and activities was telegraphed to newspapers on both sides of the Atlantic. These updates were reported with great fanfare and in great detail by British and American reporters on Barnum's payroll. And every day, copies of these updates were stuffed into rubber bags, which were inflated and thrown over the ship's side. Barnum announced that anyone finding one of these messages would win an entire day with Jumbo.

It's not clear from the available records whether any people ever claimed this prize, but if they did, they may not have enjoyed it much. The truth about Jumbo was that, contrary to the lovely picture painted by Barnum's splashy advertisements all over the United States (Jumbo—The New Darling of the American People!),

Jumbo was actually an extremely cranky, smelly, badly behaved animal. That's what many African elephants became after maturity, and it had been the main reason the Regent Park Zoo had sold him. At Regent Park he had once almost destroyed his heavily reinforced house, and twice ripped his iron chains right out of their cement footings. He had injured several of the zoo's cleaning staff, and regularly trashed his feeding bin and drinking buckets.

To calm him down, his British handlers had come up with the idea of feeding him whisky—and it had worked. That was the good news. The bad news was that over the past two years, Jumbo had become a drunk. It now took several bottles of whisky a day to keep him quiet—bottles which his handlers poured, undiluted, straight into his mouth! If whisky was unavailable, Jumbo had no objection to beer—or port wine. In fact, just about any alcoholic drink was fine with him. Unfortunately, all this drinking made him bloated, which meant he passed a great deal of gas. Bill Newman once admitted to a newsman that Jumbo farted "like a hero" and advised the man to stay a good distance upwind of him at all times.

After 13 days at sea—a time Barnum used to the fullest to stoke Jumbo-mania in the United States—the *Assyrian Monarch* arrived in New York on April 8, 1882. A huge crowd had already been waiting patiently for almost a day, entertained by Barnum's clowns and encouraged by Barnum's agents to buy more Jumbo souvenirs. When 16 horses couldn't drag Jumbo's wagon-crate up the ship's ramp, hundreds of men from the crowd joined in, and then the wagon moved slowly up Broadway, all the way to Madison Square Garden where the rest of Barnum's circus had been playing all month.

During the next four weeks, over half a million circus patrons pushed and shoved their way into the Garden to ooh and ahh over "Jumbo—The Greatest Elephant in the World!" The box office earnings covered Jumbo's entire purchase and transportion costs.

Over the next four years, and under Barnum's careful guidance—not to mention his massive, ongoing advertising campaign—Jumbo did indeed become "America's Darling." He became the main draw for The Greatest Show on Earth, helping to pull in over 12 million paying customers from all over the United States. He was surrounded by so much hype that no one seemed to notice that he was really just a very ordinary African elephant, who didn't even perform tricks like the other elephants in the circus. (African elephants were considered unteachable.) He just stood there, or walked in slow circles, while the band blared and the over-excited ringmaster bellowed out his star elephant's many supposed abilities and virtues.

Jumbo died late one night in 1885, when he refused to budge off a railroad track running next to the one on which his circus car was parked. He'd been having an off day and his handlers had fed him a lot of whisky. He was hit and killed by a passing freight train.

But that didn't mean he stopped making money for P.T. Barnum. The irrepressible showman immediately ordered a crew of taxidermists to take Jumbo's wrinkly hide, stretch it as much as they could, and stuff and mount it. The taxidermists did a splendid job, and for the next several seasons a truly gigantic version of Jumbo kept touring with the circus, amazing American children and fattening Barnum's bank account. Meanwhile Barnum published *The Life, History and Death of Jumbo*—a children's biography of Jumbo so full of inventions, exaggerations, and outright lies that it might as well have been called pure fiction. It was—of course—a best-seller for years.

Although the Jumbo public relations scam was probably Barnum's most famous, it certainly wasn't his first. By the time he bought Jumbo, Barnum had been in the entertainment business for almost 50 years and had established a well-deserved reputation as a master of flare and humbug—two elements that often overlapped.

On the flare side, his crowning glory became P.T. Barnum's Hippodrome, a spectacular $30 million amphitheater that he built in 1874. It could seat over 15,000 spectators and featured such extravagant pageants as The Sacking and Burning of Rome, a re-enactment of a true historic event that happened in 410 AD. It featured hundreds of actors dressed as Visigoths invading the ancient city of Rome, on foot and on horseback, killing and chopping up hundreds of Roman citizens and setting their entire city on fire. The realistic sets, and the smoke, flames, shrieks, and blood were so overwhelming that hundreds of spectators fled out of the hippodrome in terror.

It was the cost, and the entertainment value, of such expensive spectacles that allowed Barnum to claim that his "humbugs"—his scams—were justified. One of his earliest—the one that launched his entertainment career in 1835—was a scam involving a black slave woman named Joice Heth.

This was a time in American history when slavery was still legal, and Barnum purchased a very old slave woman whose owner claimed she had been George Washington's nurse.

To make sense of this scam, it's important to remember that George Washington was America's most idolized historical figure. He was known as the Father of America, and had been its first president. To meet a woman who had actually nurtured and raised "little Georgie," and who could tell first-hand anecdotes about his early life, would have been an experience that many Americans would have been willing to pay good money for.

The only problem was that George Washington had been born in 1732—and Joice was said to have been born in 1674. That would have made her a whopping 161 years old!

As astonishing as it seems today, people a century ago didn't think that was totally unbelievable. It seemed a stretch, certainly, but Joice Heth really did look awfully old. Her limbs were withered, and she was blind, toothless, and weighed about 23 kilograms (50 pounds). But she was also lively, talkative, and loved to sing old hymns. Barnum decided to take the chance.

He started by doing what he later became famous for—flooding New York with advertisements and handbills: FOR ONE DAY ONLY!! JOICE HETH—GEORGE WASHINGTON'S NANNY! LAST OPPORTUNITY!! DON'T MISS IT!

He then went on to invent and exaggerate outrageously. Suddenly Joice Heth was the "mother of 15 children," the youngest of whom had died several years earlier at the age of 116! The most "eminent and intelligent" physicians had examined her and pronounced her to be the age she claimed (a lie). Furthermore, the proceeds of this exhibition would be used to "buy the freedom of her five great-grandchildren" (a total lie). But tens of thousands of gullible New Yorkers took the bait.

Joice Heth, despite all her limitations, turned out to be quite a hit. She seemed to love performing (it certainly beat scrubbing floors!). She was supposed to answer questions from the audience, but mostly she just ignored them and entertained herself, telling jokes and laughing uproariously, singing hymns, and prattling on about things nobody could really understand (remember that she had no teeth).

When the crowds eventually began to thin out, Barnum doubled his ticket prices and paid reporters to announce that demand for tickets for the Joice Heth exhibition was now so high that a premium had been placed on them. That increased the size of the audience for a while longer.

Once that approach had worn out, Barnum came up with a real whopper. He began sending anonymous letters to New York's newspapers accusing himself of being a fraud! His letters made the astonishing claim that Joice Heth wasn't a live woman at all, but an automaton, a robot, made up of "whalebone, rubber and lots of springs ingeniously put together, made to move at the slightest touch of the operator!"

It sounds ridiculous, but Barnum was just making clever use of a recent event that had made newspaper headlines all over the city. A showman exhibiting a chess-playing robot (if you could beat him at the game you got your money back) had recently been exposed as a fraud when his "robot" turned out to have a dwarf hidden inside it. Now people who had seen the Joice Heth presentation began to wonder—had they missed something? Had the woman on the stage perhaps been a robot with a dwarf inside her, too?

If so, this was one amazingly convincing robot.

Thousands came back and paid another entry fee to check her out more closely.

And for Barnum, this meant more money in the bank.

Joice Heth eventually died peacefully in her sleep, about a year later. But just before giving her a very respectable burial in New York's Bethel Cemetery, Barnum allowed the famous New York surgeon Dr. David L. Rogers to do an autopsy to prove that Joice Heth really had been 161 years old. The operation was attended by a very large crowd of doctors, medical students, clergymen, newspaper reporters, and undertakers—all of whom had to pay a hefty entrance fee for the privilege. Even in death Joice Heth was still making money for P.T. Barnum!

Unfortunately the autopsy didn't turn out the way Barnum had planned. (Had he honestly thought it would??) Dr. Rogers announced that "there had to be some mistake" because this woman was only about 70 to 80 years old. Barnum protested loudly, but the damage was done. For the next several years, Barnum had to keep his name off the flyers and advertisements for various projects he undertook.

But that certainly didn't slow him down. Take the Grand Hoboken Buffalo Hunt, which Barnum staged in New Jersey on August 31, 1843. He'd come across a notice announcing the sale of a herd of buffalo for a very cheap price. On inspection, he could see why. The animals were scrawny, mangy, and starving—but they gave Barnum an idea. He bought the herd and then placed announcements in all the New York papers that a grand, historical buffalo hunt would be staged in Hoboken, New Jersey, just a short ferry ride from New York City. The hunt would be conducted by a party of genuine warrior Indians, who would risk life and limb to chase and kill these most fearsome beasts in North America. Best of all, this event would be *entirely free of charge* to the public.

This offer amazed the 25,000 spectators who poured across the Hudson River to take in the free event—until they saw the buffalo involved. The sorry critters were so tame and confused that even the "warrior Indians" couldn't seem to budge them, no matter how hard they whooped and leaped about. The crowd snickered and jeered—then finally gave up and went home, disappointed. Only Barnum ended up happy—he'd made a deal with the people who ran the ferries and the concession stands for a 50 percent share of their profits. The day had netted him a cool $30,000—and he'd been able to earn it without further risk to his reputation!

In 1869, some workmen near Cardiff, New York dug up what seemed to be a petrified giant. The body was over 3 meters (10 feet) tall and weighed 1250 kilograms (one and one-third tons). The man on whose farm the body was found—a William Newell—teamed up with his cousin George Hull to exhibit this startling discovery to the public. At first Hull charged every spectator 5 cents, but as more and more spectators arrived, he raised his price to 50 cents, then one dollar. The people just kept coming. That's when P.T. Barnum heard about it.

It didn't matter to Barnum that scientists who'd inspected the giant were already calling it a fake—nothing more than a statue hacked out of a big block of gypsum. Every cell in his showman's body told him this could be a huge money-maker. So he offered Newell and Hull the astonishing sum of $100,000 to rent—merely rent!—their giant for three months.

Hull and Newell refused.

Barnum doubled his offer. Hull and Newell still refused.

There was no way Barnum was going to take no for an answer. It simply wasn't his style. So he hired a New York sculptor to make him an exact replica of the Cardiff Giant. Then he began exhibiting the statue in his own museum in New York City.

When Newell and Hull finally ran out of audience in Cardiff, they decided to take their giant on a North American tour. First stop was New York—and that's when they discovered that their giant had already preceded them.

They promptly took Barnum to court.

For a while it looked as if this time Barnum wasn't going to get away with it. This time he'd gone too far. The Prince of Humbug was being sued for every penny he owned.

But then, just as the trial began, investigators discovered that George Hull had purchased a big block of gypsum in Iowa several years earlier. Then they found a stonecutter in Chicago who confessed to having fabricated Hull's "giant." Hull, the judge decided, was a scammer himself.

This discovery allowed Barnum to claim that all he'd done, Your Honor, was exhibit a hoax of a hoax!

Case dismissed.

To Hull's chagrin, Barnum kept right on exhibiting his "authentic fake" Cardiff Giant in his museum, and people kept right on paying him to see it, for years, even though everyone knew that it wasn't real.

"There's a sucker born every minute," Hull said disgustedly when told of Barnum's success.

It was a statement that could have been P.T. Barnum's life motto. In fact, over the years, people began crediting Barnum for having said it.

Poor George Hull. It was the most memorable thing he ever said—and in the end, P.T. Barnum robbed him of that, too.

Instant Globe-Circling: Just Add Water

ON MARCH 17, 1968, IN LONDON, ENGLAND, a great banner headline appeared in the London *Sunday Times* newspaper.

It announced the creation of a solo, nonstop, round-the-world London *Sunday Times* Golden Globe Yacht Race—the first race of its kind, and the longest, most challenging competition in the history of yachting.

No one had ever sailed single-handedly around the world without stopping at least once. The sailor who could do so in the fastest time would receive a prize of 50,000 pounds (about $100,000)!

The race was unusual in several respects. First, since it involved circling the world, contestants didn't all have to start and finish together at a single location. Anyone could enter the race from anywhere in the world—so long as they finished back where they'd started. Second, contestants could start their race anytime between June 1, 1968 and October 31, 1968. Everyone would have to keep an accurate daily logbook and be willing to have it examined by the judges at the end of the race. The winner would be determined after the final contestant had landed back in his home port.

Not surprisingly, the race attracted many of the world's most famous sailors. There was Bill Leslie King, a British ex-naval submarine commander who had won many prizes with his yacht *Galway Blazer II*. There was Robin Knox-Johnston, known worldwide for the speed of his ketch *Suhaili*. There was Bernard Moitessier, the legendary French yachtsman who held the current record for the longest nonstop solo sailing voyage in his yacht *The Joshua*.

Other veteran stars of the yachting world included British naval commander Nigel Tetley, Australian dentist Bill Howell, the British adventurers John Ridgway and Chay Blyth (who had rowed across the Atlantic Ocean together two years earlier), the Italian yachting champion Alex Carozzo, and the award-winning French yachtsman Loick Fougeron.

And then there was a mysterious contestant who was completely unknown to the yachting world. He hadn't set any records, or won any sailing trophies or prizes. All that the newspapers were able to report about this man was that his name was Donald Crowhurst, his home port was Teignmouth, England, and the name of his boat was the *Teignmouth Electron*.

The press called him the "dark horse" entrant.

Donald Crowhurst was an electronics engineer who had entered the London *Sunday Times* Golden Globe Yacht Race completely on impulse.

That didn't surprise anyone who knew Crowhurst. He was a very impulsive sort of man. Impulsive—and reckless. He was notorious for careening around his home county of Devon like a demented race-car driver. He'd smashed up three cars by the time he turned 26.

He'd even been kicked out of the Royal Air Force for roaring straight through a barracks full of sleeping men on his motorcycle, drunk as a skunk.

Yet he was very smart, and could be enormously charming. He could make you feel as if you were the most important person in the world. He was generous and funny and a lot of fun to be around. As a result, he had a lot of friends.

But even his friends rolled their eyes when they heard that Crowhurst had entered the *Sunday Times* yacht race. What on earth could he have been thinking? Crowhurst barely knew how to sail—he was a novice sailor at best. And what was all this about a boat called the *Teignmouth Electron?* Crowhurst didn't even own a boat.

"That's true, but I'm going to build one," Crowhurst grinned. "And when I do, that's what it's going to be called."

That's when his friends began questioning his sanity in all seriousness. To build an ordinary weekend sailboat from scratch in a mere six months—the time remaining until the October 31 deadline—might be a possibility, but to design, build, launch, test, tune up, and properly provision a boat for a race as grueling as the Golden Globe would take at least a year, even under the best of circumstances. It would also cost at least 50,000 pounds.

And Donald Crowhurst was broke.

This wasn't because he was lazy or didn't know how to handle money. Three years earlier he'd founded his own electronics factory, Electron Utilization, which at its height had employed 12 assemblers and been a considerable success. But Crowhurst got bored easily, and he'd gotten tired of running a business. Soon the plant was down to half a dozen assemblers; most recently only a single assembler working part-time.

His main financial backer, Stanley Best, had become alarmed and suspicious about where all his money had gone. He'd demanded a look at the books—and while he hadn't found anything dishonest, it had become clear that most of his investment had been lost.

So Stanley Best was probably the least likely human being

on Earth to lend Donald Crowhurst any more money—but Crowhurst called him anyway.

Best couldn't believe his ears. "You want money for *what?*" he demanded.

Crowhurst explained that he was desperate. He'd tried getting people to lend him their boat, and he'd tried getting shipyards to sponsor him, but he hadn't had any luck and he was running out of time. Was there any possible way at all that Best could spare him 50,000 pounds?

Best's initial reply was probably unprintable, but Crowhurst could be very persuasive. Somehow, after a series of urgent, pleading phone calls and meetings that went on over several days, Best finally agreed to put up 30,000 pounds to have a bare-bones version of the *Teignmouth Electron* built.

When Crowhurst's friends heard about this amazing development, they rallied around. If Donald could pull off this kind of miracle, he could pull off anything. Everyone pitched in and the project began to shape up. To save money and time, Crowhurst designed much of the boat himself, and hired two shipyards to build different parts of it simultaneously.

The boat Crowhurst designed was a 12.5-meter (41-foot) trimaran—a boat with three hulls, a main one in the middle and a smaller one on each side like outrigger floats. The great advantage of trimarans is that they are very fast and stable with a wind at their backs. Their weakness is that when the wind blows from the sides, they become sluggish and hard to keep on course.

Even with everyone helping, the work progressed at a frustratingly slow pace. Crowhurst worked like a maniac, 20 hours a day, negotiating, suggesting, fixing, and inventing, but he also argued with everyone, driving his helpers crazy. He haggled about the boat's design, its materials, how to fit everything together, what systems to install. For every problem he encountered, his fevered brain always seemed to come up with three half-baked solutions instead of a single workable one.

And then there were the usual bungles—hatch covers that didn't fit, equipment that didn't work, sails that were the wrong shape or size, and motors that were miswired. On a normal boat-building project you didn't worry about those things because there was time to find them, fix them, and test them. But Crowhurst and his friends didn't have the time. Some things got fixed, but some didn't. Crowhurst tried to keep a list, but he kept losing it.

On its shakedown cruise five months later—when the hastily assembled *Teignmouth Electron* was tested for the first time in sea-going conditions—so many things went wrong that she almost sank twice, and the trip took two weeks instead of the planned three days!

So it definitely seemed a miracle when, on October 31, 1968, at 4:52 p.m., only seven hours before the final cutoff, the *Teign-mouth Electron* staggered out of Teignmouth harbor to enter the London *Sunday Times* Golden Globe Yacht Race—with her paint barely dry, her cabin still littered with uninstalled nautical equipment, and a stack of unpaid bills fluttering in her wake.

Not surprisingly, her start was not great. On November 2, Crowhurst radioed a Morse Code message (which was the way sailors communicated in those days) to Rodney Hallworth, his press agent for the race, that the *Teignmouth Electron*'s self-steering gear was falling apart and that one of her outrigger floats was filling with water. SPENDING MUCH TIME FIXING LEAKS, REPAIRING EQUIPMENT AND BAILING, he reported. HEADWINDS KEEPING PROGRESS DOWN TO 75 MILES PER DAY.

On November 5, Crowhurst radioed again. GENERATOR FAILED. USING BATTERIES, RUNNING LOW. Then nothing. No radio transmissions for almost two weeks.

When Crowhurst began transmitting again, on November 16, he announced that he had managed to fix his generator, but that crosswinds were slowing him down. He reported his position as just off the coast of Portugal, heading for the island of Madeira.

He was now managing less than 50 nautical miles per day—the slowest sailing speed of any of the race contestants. His progress was so poor that the betting shops in England didn't even bother calculating the odds for Donald Crowhurst.

Finally, a month after setting sail, the *Teignmouth Electron* began to pick up speed.

So far, Crowhurst had been bucking westerlies—winds that blew from the side, to which trimarans don't respond well. Now he had finally sailed far enough into the Atlantic Ocean to catch the northeast trade winds—winds that blew from behind.

The effect was immediate. The *Teignmouth Electron* surged ahead and began to make rapid progress. On December 10 Crowhurst radioed that he had just finished a week of 145 to 174 sea miles per day—including one 24-hour period in which he'd managed a whopping 243 nautical miles. TUNING TRIALS OVER! he radioed cheerfully. RACE BEGINS!

He was now halfway between Africa and South America in the mid-Atlantic, with a thousand-mile sail straight down to the tip of Africa ahead of him, and the wind at his back all the way. This was where trimarans really shone. AVERAGING 170 MILES DAILY, he radioed on December 14. APPROACHING TRISTAN DA CUNHA ISLAND, he reported on December 20. On Christmas Eve, in a radio message forwarded by an operator in South Africa, he reported he was already rounding the Cape of Good Hope.

Suddenly the betting shops in England sat up and began to take notice. What was happening here? The *Teignmouth Electron* was beginning to move like a racehorse!

Rodney Hallworth and the rest of Crowhurst's friends in Teignmouth couldn't believe their luck. They'd been so bogged down in gloom, convinced their boat was a total loser, that it had taken them some time to realize what was happening. They became even more amazed when it was announced that Crowhurst's 243 nautical miles in a 24-hour period might just possibly be a world record!

"Donald Crowhurst, last man out in the *Sunday Times* round-the-world yacht race, covered a breathtaking and possibly record-breaking 243 miles in his 41-foot trimaran *Teignmouth Electron* last Sunday," the *Sunday Times* reported. "The achievement is even more remarkable considering the very poor speeds in the first three weeks of his voyage. He took longer to reach the Cape Verdes than any other competitor..."

Another factor that significantly improved the *Teignmouth Electron*'s position in the race was a string of unbelievably bad luck that had dogged many of the other contestants during the previous weeks.

Ridgway, Blyth, and Howell had all been forced to drop out with mechanical problems. Bill King's *Galway Blazer II* had lost its mast in a south Atlantic storm and was being towed back to Cape Town. Alex Carozzo had developed a stomach ulcer and had given up. Loick Fougeron had capsized in the Roaring Forties—the stormy region between 40 and 50 degrees of latitude south—and had quit the race. Robin Knox-Johnston had capsized in the Tasman Sea but had managed to right his boat and was carrying on—however, a lot of his gear had been smashed and his sails were in tatters. Only Nigel Tetley and Bernard Moitessier were still in good shape and sailing steadily, though neither was managing to match Crowhurst's speed.

KNOX–JOHNSTON LEADS, Hallworth radioed Crowhurst excitedly. MOITESSIER BEYOND TASMANIA. TETLEY EASTERN INDIAN OCEAN. YOUR AVERAGE SPEED 30 MILES FASTER. PLEASE GIVE WEEKLY POSITION AND MILEAGE. CHEERS, RODNEY.

Crowhurst agreed, and sent at least four more reports. Each time, his odds in the race improved.

Then, on January 20, 1969, he reported more generator trouble. His last transmission was on January 21.

For the next three weeks, Hallworth kept sending radio queries to the *Teignmouth Electron* but received no reply. He complained to Crowhurst's wife Clare that he was just getting dead air. Was she getting anything on her radio?

Nobody was—but at first no one got too worried about it. Crowhurst's generator had caused problems right from the start, and so far he'd always managed to fix it. But after another three weeks of dead air, everyone started wondering. By now, barring any signficant problems, Crowhurst should have been somewhere in the Tasman Sea, sailing east between Australia and New Zealand, but no naval traffic was reporting him there.

There was also no sign of Knox-Johnston, who had been out of radio contact even longer, but who had occasionally been sighted by a passing freighter or airplane. Now no one had reported seeing him for several weeks, and people were beginning to fear that he might be out of the race, or even drowned.

Bernard Moitessier was still cruising right along—but then, on April 2, to everyone's utter astonishment, the London *Sunday Times* received a letter from him, mailed from Tahiti, explaining that he'd had such a great time sailing through the South Pacific that he'd decided life was too short to spend it racing around the globe. He was dropping out of the race to spend some quality time among the South Pacific islands!

That left only Nigel Tetley, who had rounded Cape Horn on March 20 and was now heading north in a beeline for home.

Two weeks later, on April 6, a tanker spotted Robin Knox-Johnston in the middle of the Atlantic Ocean. His boat was a mess and his speed was very slow—but he was still sailing valiantly.

Only Crowhurst remained unaccounted for. His odds in the betting shops of England dropped lower and lower.

But then, on April 9, over 10 weeks since his last radio message, a very faint signal from the *Teignmouth Electron* was relayed to England via a radio station in Argentina. It read: HEADING DIGGER RAMREZ.

This news brought everybody right back to the edge of their seats!

Digger Ramrez was sailor talk for Diego Ramírez, a small island just southwest of Cape Horn. If Crowhurst was closing in on Diego Ramirez, it meant he had already sailed all the way around the bottom of the world—through the South Atlantic Ocean, the Indian Ocean, the Tasman Sea, and the South Pacific Ocean—and was now coming around the bottom of South America on the last leg of his return journey.

Not only that, but it also meant he'd been belting along at a very high speed—about 178 nautical miles per day. If he could keep that up, he might well beat the current leader, Nigel Tetley, and actually win the race.

Crowhurst's home team in Teignmouth leaped off their seats and started screaming. This was incredible! One minute their man was dead last, then he was setting world records, then he disappeared completely, and now he was chasing the leader—how was this going to end?

YOU'RE ONLY TWO WEEKS BEHIND TETLEY! Hallworth radioed Crowhurst. PHOTO FINISH WILL MAKE GREAT NEWS! RODNEY.

On April 18 Crowhurst radioed confirmation that he'd rounded Cape Horn and was passing the Falkland Islands east of Argentina.

The news sent Nigel Tetley's support team into a near panic. For the past several weeks their man had looked like the clear winner, and now, at the last moment, there seemed to be a chance that victory could be snatched away from him. His boat—a trimaran very similar to Crowhurst's—was suffering from similar problems: leaking floats, peeling fiberglas, damaged running gear. He'd been babying it along, trying not to sail too aggressively, hoping he could keep it all in one piece during the final month's sailing.

But when they did the math, the Tetley team could see that at his current rate of speed, Tetley wouldn't make it. He was simply not sailing fast enough. If he couldn't do better than 140 nautical miles per day, Donald Crowhurst would win the race.

Tetley decided to go for broke. He began to sail as hard as he possibly could. He strained his equipment to the utmost, desperately squeezing another 20 nautical miles per day out of his boat. At 20 additional miles, his calculations showed, he might be able to win the race by a hair.

Meanwhile, Crowhurst was having his troubles too. SIX BROKEN FRAMES, he radioed on May 12. TWO FOOT SPLIT STARBOARD FLOAT TOPSIDES.

After a week of speeds reaching up to 200 miles per day, Crowhurst reported unhappily: FOUR DAYS LOST, UNUSUAL NORTH-EASTERLY GALE. OVERTAKE TETLEY ONLY BY LUCK NOW.

But by the third week of May, with Tetley approaching the Canary Islands and Crowhurst just off Brazil, the gamblers in England were putting their money on Crowhurst.

In Teignmouth, the excitement was really starting to heat up. Hallworth booked Teignmouth's largest meeting hall and was preparing the biggest, noisiest celebration in the town's history. Win or lose, Crowhurst had already achieved amazing success. He, a weekend sailor, a novice, a beginner, had already beaten eight of the world's top-ranked sailors—the cream of the yachting world! TEIGNMOUTH AGOG AT YOUR WONDERS! Hallworth radioed Crowhurst. WHOLE TOWN PLANNING HUGE WELCOME. RODNEY.

And then, just after midnight on May 21, it happened.

Sailing frantically through a storm near the Azores Islands, with too much sail laid on, one of Nigel Tetley's already cracked floats finally broke away and smashed into his boat's center hull.

The resulting hole was so big that Tetley couldn't plug it. As the water poured in, he had just enough time to radio an SOS giving his position, launch his liferaft, and row clear.

His boat sank in minutes.

He was rescued the next day by a British naval vessel.

Hearing the report, the world's news media went berserk.

What a story this would be! A complete unknown takes to the high seas in an unfinished boat, challenging the world's most famous and experienced sailors in a global yacht race, and six months and 26,000 nautical miles later, cleans their clocks!

Now all Donald Crowhurst had to do was loaf the last 4,000 miles to his home port of Teignmouth, collect his prize, and spend the rest of his days awash in fame and fortune.

MORE THAN A HUNDRED THOUSAND PEOPLE EXPECTED TO GIVE YOU A HERO'S WELCOME WHEN YOU ARRIVE! Hallworth radioed Crowhurst. He was planning at least a week's worth of feasts, celebrations, and other public events. There would be an international tour, interviews with the world's top journalists, and lots of commercial endorsements. Hallworth's phone was already ringing off the hook.

Oddly enough, Crowhurst didn't seem all that thrilled about his luck. He seemed a lot more preoccupied with all the mechanical and electrical problems he was having. Like Tetley's, his floats had been taking on more and more water, and since somebody had forgotten to install the suction hoses on his bailing pumps, he had to do all the bailing by hand. His steering gear was giving him endless trouble, and his radio transmitter kept cutting out. He suspected that sooner or later it would cut out completely.

His suspicion proved to be true. After June 1, Hallworth received no more radio messages from the *Teignmouth Electron*.

Fortunately, this time the world didn't lose sight of Donald Crowhurst. He had meanwhile crossed the equator and was now sailing in the more crowded shipping lanes of the North Atlantic Ocean. Various freighters and ocean liners reported seeing the *Teignmouth Electron* as she moved steadily northward.

Piecing together the various reports, the race judges in London began to notice a strange thing.

The *Teignmouth Electron* seemed to be sailing slower and slower. Some days she was barely covering 20 nautical miles. In fact, Crowhurst wasn't even using his mainsail anymore—just his much smaller jibsail.

Then Crowhurst entered the Sargasso Sea, and that's when the *Teignmouth Electron* really began to slow down. The Sargasso Sea is a strange phenomenon—a huge, eerily heaving expanse of floating seaweed in the middle of the Atlantic Ocean. It's also known for its calm weather—sailboats often have trouble getting enough wind to pass through all those weeds.

Now Crowhurst was barely making 5 miles per day.

Hallworth and his crew weren't paying much attention to Crowhurst's affairs at sea because they had their hands full handling his affairs on land. So many offers and requests were now pouring in that Hallworth had to rent a second office, hire a secretary, and put in another phone line. Officials at Buckingham Palace called on behalf of the Queen's husband, Prince Philip, asking whether Crowhurst would be willing to present the annual Duke of Edinburgh Awards next year. The post office called, offering to produce a special Crowhurst stamp. Hallworth had already printed 10,000 postcards featuring a photograph of "Donald Crowhurst, winner of the London *Sunday Times* Golden Globe Yacht Race," and was sending them all over the world on behalf of the Teignmouth Chamber of Commerce. The cards read: GREETINGS FROM TEIGNMOUTH, THE DEVON RESORT CHOSEN BY DONALD CROWHURST FOR HIS TRIUMPHANT AROUND-THE-WORLD YACHT RACE!

And then, on the evening of July 10, two policemen arrived at the Crowhurst residence to bring Clare disastrous news. Early that morning the Royal Mail vessel *Picardy*, en route from London to the Caribbean, had almost hit a trimaran floating aimlessly in the Sargasso Sea.

It was the *Teignmouth Electron*—the crew had recognized her from all the publicity. She was still seaworthy, there was plenty of food in her galley, and her liferaft was still onboard—but Donald Crowhurst had disappeared.

After days of futile searching by both the British and the American navies, attention turned to the *Teignmouth Electron*'s logbook.

That's when the answer began to emerge.

They found not one logbook, but three.

Logbook #1 recorded a journey that went all around the

world. Logbook #2 recorded a journey that was centered mainly in the South Atlantic Ocean. Logbook #3 was more of a notebook, containing freighters' radio reports of sea and weather conditions all along the route described in Logbook #1.

It didn't take the judges long to figure out what had happened.

Donald Crowhurst had never sailed the *Teignmouth Electron* around the world. He had merely sailed into the middle of the Atlantic Ocean, then sailed in circles while only *reporting* a journey around the world—by radio.

Logbook #2 made it clear how this had happened. Crowhurst hadn't originally intended to fake his journey, but by December 1, 1968, it had become obvious that the *Teignmouth Electron* was in no shape to sail the much rougher waters of the Indian Ocean and the Tasman Sea. Her hulls were leaking so badly, she was taking on massive amounts of seawater every day. Her wiring was a mess and her navigational equipment a disaster. One good storm would have sunk her. Indeed, during his six months at sea, Crowhurst had at one point been forced to land on the coast of Argentina to make emergency repairs.

That's when the idea of a "virtual journey" had occurred to him. It was the days before satellites, before radio operators could pinpoint exactly where a radio message had come from. All Crowhurst had to do was report faked positions along his round-the-world route, listen to marine weather reports from those locations, and incorporate those reports into a fake logbook. Result: a logbook that would look accurate and believable when checked against the official records of weather and sea conditions around the world from December 1, 1968 to mid-May, 1969.

Having believable entries was important, because Crowhurst suspected that his high sailing speed of 170 to 200 nautical miles per day, after his miserable 50 miles per day at the beginning, would make the judges suspicious. He was right: one of the judges had already sent a letter to the race chairman, urging him to make sure Crowhurst's logbook was carefully verified.

But as the race neared its end and Crowhurst found himself neck-and-neck with one of the most experienced yachtsmen in the world, he became less and less certain that his logbook would fool navigational experts.

So he hatched an ingenious back-up scheme. He wouldn't try winning the race. He'd arrange to come in second!

This would solve two problems with one stroke. Coming in second against one of the greatest sailors in the world was no shame. In fact, Crowhurst would still look like a hero. But a second-place finisher's logbook would probably not be examined very carefully. And that's what Crowhurst wanted.

Which was why, when Nigel Tetley's trimaran sank in a storm near the Azores, Crowhurst wasn't overjoyed—he was devastated.

As the winner, he would be unable to avoid the kind of scrutiny he feared—and its inevitable results. Shame. Dishonor. Humiliation. Disgrace.

As he neared the end of his journey, he sailed more and more slowly, frantically turning the problem over in his mind. What to do? What to do? How could he escape this looming disaster?

Finally, at 10:03 on the morning of July 1, in the middle of the Sargasso Sea, he felt ready to answer that question.

"I will resign the game at 11:20 today," he wrote in his notebook.

Those were his last words.

At 11:20 a.m. on July 1, 1969, the race judges concluded, Crowhurst stepped off the deck of the *Teignmouth Electron* and drowned.

Operation Bernhard

EARLY ON THE MORNING OF MAY 13, 1945, a fisherman who had just left his house on the shore of Traun Lake in western Austria came pounding back up the stairs.

"Wake up! Wake up, everybody! Come out here! You won't believe this!"

His half-awake family stumbled into their yard and gazed out at the water in astonishment.

The little lake was totally covered by a gently bobbing blanket of thousands of British banknotes!

Several other fishermen appeared. They ran back to call their families. A crowd of friends and neighbors gathered quickly. Soon hundreds of fully dressed villagers were thrashing about in the lake, frantically stuffing sodden banknotes into pails and baskets. The air was filled with delighted shrieks, gasps, and exclamations.

Some rushed home to dry their money in ovens or on stovetops. Others laid out the bills on the beach and in a nearby field to dry in the sun.

"Where on earth did this money come from?" asked a fisherman. "Somebody must have robbed a bank!" said his wife. "But why are they British banknotes? Why aren't they Austrian?" a neighbor demanded.

"Never mind all that," someone pointed out. "The most important question is: are the bills counterfeit or are they genuine?"

The last question seemed easiest to answer. Several people

hurried over to the nearby town of Endsee, to the village bank. A cashier tested the sample bill with ultraviolet light and passed it around among her colleagues for their opinions.

Everyone agreed: the bill was genuine.

By this time a squad of American soldiers had arrived at the lake to take control of the situation. Since World War II had ended only a week earlier, most of western Europe was under Allied military occupation. The Americans roped off the area and tried to keep everyone out, but since there were still banknotes floating on the lake, this proved to be difficult.

Despite the soldiers' best efforts to scoop them out, more and more bills kept floating to the surface. Eventually a fisherman suggested that the source had to be farther upstream. He said the bills were probably being carried into the lake by the Traun River.

The source was soon discovered: a dozen wooden cases filled with banknotes, which had been flung into the river a short distance above the lake. The cases had burst, and were slowly releasing their contents into the swift-flowing current.

But there was also a second astounding discovery—an abandoned German Security Service transport truck near Gmunden, a 20-minute drive farther north. It was filled with 23 similar cases. They too proved to be bursting with British banknotes—hundreds of thousands of them.

This was becoming too big for the local American commandant. He rang up U.S. military headquarters in Germany. Soon radio and telephone messages were flashing back and forth between Frankfurt and Washington, Washington and London. The FBI, Scotland Yard, and the Bank of England were alerted. Forgery experts from all three countries jumped into airplanes and trucks and hurried to Traun Lake to investigate.

It took them years to do it, but what Allied investigators eventually uncovered was Operation Bernhard—the biggest banknote counterfeiting operation in the history of the world.

Operation Bernhard was first proposed to Germany's Fuehrer, Adolf Hitler, by members of his Security Service (Reichsicherheitsdienst) back in 1939. That was shortly after Germany had started World War II by attacking and seizing Bohemia, Moravia, and Poland.

In response, Britain, an ally of Poland, had declared war on Germany.

Instead of invading Britain, the German Security Service thought they might be able to beat the British more easily by the ingenious method of flooding the world with millions of fake British banknotes. This would have the effect of making Britain's currency so suspect it would become almost worthless, which in turn would cause the British economy to collapse. With a collapsed economy Britain would no longer be able to continue the war, and this would force her to surrender.

Hitler didn't much like the idea—he felt the German Reich (Empire) didn't need to win a war by using such "dishonorable" means—but he agreed to a smaller version of Operation Bernhard. Since he was already planning to attack many more countries (Holland, Belgium, France, Russia, and more), he knew Germany would need a lot of spies. Counterfeit banknotes, he determined, could be used to pay for Germany's foreign intelligence system— its spies, collaborators, and foreign agents—but nothing else.

The man chosen for the operation—and after whom it was codenamed—was Bernhard Krueger, the head of the Security Service's Forgery Division. This division produced fake passports and other bogus identity papers for Germany's spies.

Krueger was a little different from the other Nazi officials who ran the Security Service. He was really more interested in typography than politics. He loved the world of printing, and preferred messing around with blocks of type and fine papers to attending endless political meetings. And even though he was as meticulous and organized as the rest of his colleagues, he also had a sense of humor. Some of the other officers didn't like that very much.

Krueger was eager to get started, but there was an immediate problem: manpower. To get Operation Bernhard rolling he needed dozens of highly specialized craftsmen—printers, composers, engravers, chemists, papermakers, banking experts. Trying to find people of this kind who weren't already fully employed in the war effort was going to be a huge headache.

Suddenly Krueger had a brainwave. He knew that some of Germany's brightest and most accomplished scientists were wasting away in the country's own concentration camps. Why not offer the work to them?

The inmates of these political prison camps were not criminals. The camps were simply the Nazis' way of getting rid of anyone they considered politically unacceptable—homosexuals, gypsies, political opponents, and especially Jews, whom Hitler blamed for all of Germany's economic troubles. Here, prisoners were brutally treated, forced to work long hours at hard labor, and kept on starvation rations. The death rate was staggering.

In his proposal to his bosses, Krueger insisted that his workers would have to be given decent accommodation, proper food, and a lot more privileges than was the norm. His superiors were appalled at the idea and grumbled about it for quite a while. However, since there was no other source of such specialized labor for Operation Bernhard, they eventually agreed.

Several hundred men volunteered from throughout the concentration camp system, and Krueger selected 40 of them. About half were Jewish, nearly all were non-German (Czech, Hungarian, Polish, etc.), and only one had actual counterfeiting experience. Krueger gathered them all at Sachsenhausen prison, northeast of Berlin, where he built them a separately guarded compound designated Block 19. This compound had heated rooms, washing facilities, and separate bunks for the workers—unheard-of luxuries compared to regular concentration camp conditions.

Most other concentration camp inmates considered "Krueger's men," as they came to be called, outrageously lucky, and most of Krueger's men felt that way too, but some had mixed feelings about their new job. It was true that if the Germans needed a prisoner's skills, they weren't as likely to kill, starve, or beat him. On the other hand, working for Operation Bernhard meant working directly to help the Nazis win the war. Some felt conflicted about that.

It certainly helped that Krueger was a fair-minded, likable man who was interested only in their skills, not their religion, sexual orientation, or political opinions.

But Krueger probably wouldn't have been able to get away with civilized treatment of his men if Operation Bernhard hadn't been so top-secret. The secrecy rating of Block 19 was so high that only Krueger, Block 19's special guards, and the prison commandant knew what the inmates were actually doing in there.

The work they now began involved an enormous challenge. British banknotes were widely believed to be impossible to forge. Their engravings were said to be too complex and intricate to duplicate. After the men had spent several hours carefully examining the various banknotes under a large magnifying table, Krueger offered to make things easier by having them produce only British five-pound notes.

Everyone was relieved.

But when the engravers showed Krueger their first efforts, he shook his head. They weren't bad, but side by side with a genuine bill they didn't look the same. They had to look identical—so perfectly identical that they would still appear legitimate even when magnified 20 times their normal size.

The bills had to be so perfect that even the Bank of England would accept them, Krueger insisted. It would be hard—but possible.

Krueger's men went back to try again.

The papermakers were having problems, too. Krueger had sent several genuine banknotes to a laboratory for analysis, and the lab had sent back a list of the paper's ingredients, but when Krueger's men copied it, the result just didn't feel right. The paper felt too stiff.

Two weeks later Krueger's phone rang. "We've got it!" a papermaker announced. It had been the flax. The flax the British used in their paper came from Turkey.

Krueger ordered his assistant to get some flax from Turkey.

There was an embarrassed silence. "Herr Krueger—Germany is also at war with Turkey," the man said finally.

Krueger laughed. "How inconvenient," he said. "We'll have to smuggle it in. We'll get some through Italy—call it emergency medical supplies. Or are we at war with Italy, too?"

When the Turkish flax arrived, it definitely helped—but the match was still not perfect.

What could it be? After months of digging, the papermakers discovered that the British use recycled linen in their paper. Krueger's papermakers had been using only new material.

Krueger was pleased. He ordered his linen sent to nearby factories as rags, with instructions to have them all returned after use and cleaned, then added to the paper mix. That did the trick!

A third problem involved Krueger's method of aging the bank-notes.

Clean, freshly printed banknotes are more likely to arouse suspicion than used, old ones. To age his banknotes in a hurry, Krueger got half a dozen men to fold, crumple, and generally "work" the bills with unclean hands to remove their new look.

That was good, but left one clue—the engravings remained too sharp-edged. In an old banknote, the oils in the ink have soaked into the paper, giving the engravings a slightly blurry outline. A used banknote with sharply outlined engravings didn't make sense. It might fool an ordinary customer, but not an inspector from the Bank of England. After testing all sorts of chemical combinations, Krueger finally found one that caused his ink to release its oils more quickly. This made his banknotes look several years old after only a few days in the dryer.

They were getting ever closer to success.

Krueger's final problem was figuring out how to number the bills. All banknotes carry a date, a letter and number designation, and the printed signature of the Bank of England's Chief Cashier at the time of printing. Krueger had to find out how many five-pound banknotes the Bank of England had issued during the past 20 years, what their designations had been, and whose signature they had carried.

It seemed like an impossible job—but the ministry's secret agents returned with the correct information in less than two months.

Now it was all systems go!

Two weeks later, an assistant dropped the first batch of 100 care-fully dried, instantly aged, totally bogus British five-pound banknotes onto Krueger's desk.

Krueger picked one up reverently. He held it up to the light, examined it under his magnifying glass from every angle. Then he compared it to a genuine British five-pound note he kept in his desk.

"Perfect," he murmured contentedly. "This looks perfect. Now for the final test."

An agent was dispatched to Switzerland (which was neutral in the war) with a small bundle of the fake notes. Following Krueger's instructions, the agent approached a cashier in a large Zurich bank and handed her the bundle. He explained that he was worried that these bills, which he'd recently received from a client, might be counterfeit. He asked for her opinion.

The clerk asked him to have a seat.

When she returned a few minutes later, she cheerfully informed him that the notes were genuine. There was nothing to worry about.

"Are you quite certain?" the agent demanded. "I have reason to be concerned about this client's honesty."

The clerk assured him that she was quite certain. The bank had its own expert on staff, and he had inspected the notes personally.

The agent sighed. "Please don't be offended," he said. "I'm about to embark on a rather large business deal with this client, and I would sleep better if his honesty was confirmed at the highest level. Would you be so kind as to forward a sample note to the Bank of England in London? I believe they offer an authentication service."

The clerk's pleasant manner vanished. She took back the bundle and told the agent to return in two weeks.

Seventeen days later the clerk handed over a package from the Bank of England.

The banknotes had passed with flying colors.

When Krueger heard the news, he happily ordered his men to start the presses. Immediately. And for the end of the day, to celebrate, he told his assistant to round up some champagne.

His assistant looked horrified. Champagne? In a prison camp? Was Herr Krueger perhaps forgetting that these men were "enemies of the German Reich"?

Krueger grimaced. This was technically true—and Krueger seemed to be the only man in Sachsenhausen who kept forgetting it.

The purpose of counterfeiting banknotes is to try to trade fake notes for real ones. To do this, a counterfeitor might take his fake British banknotes to a bank and trade them for genuine American dollars. Or he might use them to buy valuables such as jewels, precious metals, or art for later resale.

Most counterfeitors print up as many banknotes as they think they can "sell" in a given area (usually a single city, sometimes several cities at once), then hire a small army of agents to dump the entire print run into the money stream at one go—so fast that by the time the banks wake up to the problem, everyone's long gone. This method is based on the assumption that the forgeries will be discovered quite quickly—which they usually are.

The amazing feature of Operation Bernhard was that the counterfeits made by Krueger's men were so perfect, and so unlikely to be detected, that the German Security Service could expect to dump thousands of them into the money stream at a time—and *keep* dumping in thousands more for many, many months, or even years.

Furthermore, Operation Bernhard wasn't limited to a single city, or even a group of cities. Being a government operation, it had the resources to distribute its banknotes all over the world.

So Krueger proceeded to organize his men into a production line that was soon printing more than a hundred thousand fake British five-pound notes every single month.

To find a salesman who could keep up with that level of production, the Security Service had to go outside its own organization. The job fell to Friedrich Schwend, a self-made German businessman. Schwend had begun his working life as an ordinary garage mechanic and was now a wealthy aristocrat, with mansions, yachts, and bank accounts all over the world.

Schwend was a charmer—tall, elegant, a knockout with the ladies, an enthusiastic sportsman—but above all an extraordinarily smart and efficient businessman. He belonged to the old school, which operated on the premise that in any business deal, both sides should always make a profit. This made him many friends, and assured him of a never-ending supply of customers. He kept agents in over 20 cities around the world, including Rome, Stockholm, Madrid, Budapest, Tangier, Paris, New York, Hong Kong, Amsterdam, Belgrade, and Copenhagen.

With such a network, Schwend had no trouble at all keeping up with Krueger's rate of production. In fact, it wasn't long before he was sending him impatient telegrams: NEED MORE BANKNOTES URGENTLY, STOP. MY AGENTS FINDING MANY WILLING BUYERS, STOP. CAN BARELY KEEP UP WITH DEMAND, STOP.

His success wasn't altogether surprising. First, it was now 1943, and Germany was beginning to lose the war. Its resources were stretched to the limit. Since fewer and fewer countries were accepting German banknotes (Deutschmarks) for business transactions, Schwend was often required—despite Hitler's original instructions—to use the fake British banknotes to purchase military equipment.

Second, with Germany faltering and England recovering, the

British pound was rapidly becoming the most sought-after currency in the world.

Krueger asked Schwend how many banknotes he needed.

"Three hundred thousand," Schwend suggested. "No, five hundred thousand. I could use a *million* banknotes if you could print that many!"

Krueger said he'd see what could be done.

"And why bother with five-pound notes," Schwend continued. "Why not print fifties? It's the same amount of work."

"I'll think about it," Krueger replied.

The next day, Krueger ordered his engravers to begin work on a British 50-pound note.

By early 1944, Operation Bernhard had more than tripled in size. Krueger had increased its staff to 142 men, and had added a whole new compound, called Block 18, to its quarters at Sachsenhausen prison.

Krueger's men were now pumping out half a million banknotes per month in British tens, twenties, and fifties.

Despite this, Schwend kept complaining that Krueger's men were too slow. But Krueger knew that if they printed any faster the quality would suffer—and he hated to release anything but perfect bills. If the quality suffered, the counterfeits might be detected and their agents might be caught.

Schwend wasn't concerned about that. He told Krueger about what happened to their agent in Madrid. This agent had traded Krueger's bills for Spanish pesetas, then sent the pesetas to Lisbon to trade them for genuine British notes. When the money got back to Schwend, he discovered he'd been paid in Krueger's own counterfeit banknotes! "They're so good, even some of us can't always detect our own fakes!" he chortled.

Krueger was so pleased by this story that he requested military Good Service medals, 2nd Class, for all his men at Sachsenhausen prison.

The prison officials couldn't believe their ears. The commandant asked Krueger if he'd gone totally mad. Military medals for *prisoners!?*

Krueger assured him that he was quite sane. He felt his men had earned them. They were working a lot of extra hours these days. "Please submit my request to the Medals Commission," he insisted.

Shortly after the men got their medals (which cost Krueger a lot of favors), the commandant complained to Krueger that his men were actually wearing those medals around camp.

Krueger stared at him, perplexed. This was a problem?

Of course it was a problem, the commandant said. It was upsetting the guards. Nobody had given *them* any medals. They felt Krueger's men were thumbing their noses at them.

To keep the peace, Krueger asked his men to wear their medals only during the day in their print shops.

By the summer of 1944, banknote production at Sachsenhausen was approaching a million British banknotes per month.

So many Krueger counterfeits were now in circulation worldwide that in some countries—such as Yugoslavia, Bulgaria, and Romania, where Schwend's agents had been particularly busy—Krueger's fake British currency had actually *replaced* the national currency.

In Italy, invading Allied troops were astonished to discover that store owners routinely quoted their prices in British pounds instead of Italian liras.

Even the Bank of England had by now become aware that its money supply had mysteriously grown, but the confusions of a world war and the high quality of the counterfeits made it impossible to do much about it. The bank's warnings to the forgery investigators of the world's biggest banks were largely ignored.

As Germany's armament factories were increasingly destroyed by Allied bombing, the Security Service used more and more of its counterfeit money to buy arms abroad.

In fact, Schwend informed Krueger, for the best deals in weapons, he really should be printing American dollars. American dollars were going to be the next hot currency.

Krueger said he'd have to think about it.

Only three months later—just before Christmas 1944—Krueger's men began printing a line of fake American hundred-dollar banknotes, too.

And by January 1945, working even more extra hours at a frantic pace, Krueger's men were producing about 10,000 American counterfeits per month—in *addition* to their monthly quota of British counterfeits!

But it was too late to make much difference to the Nazi war effort. Germany was crumbling, and the war was almost over. As the Russian army broke through Germany's last eastern defences and began to overrun the country, panic set in. One morning just before dawn, a group of Nazi SS troops came crashing through the doors of Blocks 18 and 19. "Everybody up! Get dressed! Line up!"

Bleary-eyed, terrified, Krueger's men stumbled to their feet.

"We want all this equipment smashed!" one of the soldiers ordered. "Anything wooden, burn it. Anything metal, cut it up or smash it. Now move!"

Everyone paled. This had been their greatest fear—the fear that when all was lost, the Germans would smash everything, kill the prisoners, destroy the records, and flee. There were rumors that this had already happened in some of the prisons farther east.

Fortunately, cooler heads prevailed. After a hurried argument, the soldiers decided this equipment was too valuable to smash. "All right! Change of plans! Everything gets packed up! Everything in boxes, cases! Hop to it!"

It took most of the day to load the trucks. They left just before dark in a 14-truck convoy, the men wedged in wherever there was room. It was the middle of winter, a bitter wind was blowing, and no one had been issued a jacket or blankets. The roads were full of refugees and bomb craters.

After three miserable days of almost no food or sleep, the convoy reached Mauthausen concentration camp in northern Austria. Its commandant was surprised and annoyed—he had no room for Krueger's men, and no rations to feed them. He had barely enough food for his own prisoners.

After an hour of heated negotiations, the men were quartered in the only room left—the camp's Execution Block. It was a huge, freezing, windowless concrete bunker, its walls pockmarked with thousands of bullet holes—and that's where an appalled Krueger finally found his men six weeks later, sick, desperately hungry, and demoralized.

Some Gestapo opponents of Operation Bernhard, accusing Krueger of being a "Jew lover" (a crime punishable by death in wartime Germany), had managed to have him reassigned without warning. It had taken him six weeks of struggling with the military bureaucracy to fight his way back to his men.

Krueger immediately arranged for a train to transfer his men out of Mauthausen and into new quarters at the nearby Redel-Zipf prison. Here they were once again provided with heated rooms, running water, and cooking and washing facilities. Relieved, the men began rebuilding their workshop.

But only two months later the American army invaded Austria from the west. With enemy troops closing in rapidly and Krueger unable to get back from a meeting in Berlin, Krueger's most recent second-in-command, Lieutenant Hansch, decided it was time to shut Operation Bernhard down for good.

The men were called together and ordered to pack up their workshop one last time. Then, according to strict orders from Krueger, they would receive their freedom.

When the last of four large army trucks had been loaded with Operation Bernhard's equipment, printing plates, and remaining counterfeit bills, army transports were ordered to take the men to nearby Ebensee prison for a handover to the Red Cross. (Two days later the Americans liberated Ebensee, and the men were freed.)

Hansch and his four Security Service trucks, meanwhile, disappeared into the night.

What happened to Hansch and his convoy took Allied inspectors years to unravel.

After most of a night's traveling over steep mountain roads, one of the trucks broke an axle near the town of Gmunden and had to be abandoned. (This was the truck the investigators discovered soon after British counterfeit banknotes first floated to the surface in Traun Lake.)

Half a day later, a second truck—one filled entirely with counterfeit British banknotes packed in wooden cases—skidded into a ditch beside the Traun River and the drivers couldn't get it back onto the road. For some reason Hansch decided to dump this truck's contents into the river. (This truck, since it was still roadworthy, was probably recommissioned by Allied forces a few days later—in any case, it was never found by the investigators.)

The remaining two trucks made it all the way to a military

research station near the town of Grundlsee before running out of fuel.

The commanding officer at the research station listened to Hansch's description of his cargo and agreed that absolute secrecy was called for. His engineers suggested wrapping everything in waterproof containers and lowering them to the bottom of a nearby lake—the Toplitzsee—that the station had been using to test various underwater weapons.

When a witness finally confessed this information to Allied investigators in late 1945, British divers were sent to the lake but found nothing. However, repeated attempts over the next 14 years finally led to success.

A team of German divers located some of the waterproof containers in 1959, producing another king's ransom in counterfeit British banknotes. To everyone's amazement, they were still in perfect condition, and were turned over to the Bank of England. More recently, in the year 2000, additional dives turned up even more banknotes and Security Service records.

As for Friedrich Schwend, he spent a brief time in an American prisoner-of-war camp in Germany, then moved to Peru, where he continued his free-wheeling business practices in partnership with various German war criminals. He also engaged in intelligence work for the U.S. Central Intelligence Agency and the Peruvian Secret Service.

Bernhard Krueger disappeared from Germany after he was accused of responsibility for the deaths of six of his men due to illness during his management of Operation Bernhard. The complaints, however, were dismissed. Krueger returned to Germany in 1956 and died there of old age at some point in the 1980s.

As for Operation Bernhard's counterfeit British and American banknotes, they were never officially withdrawn because they were simply too difficult to identify. This was a first in the history of counterfeiting—not surprising for what turned out to be the world's most sophisticated and successful counterfeiting scam.

Crazy about Books

THOMAS WILLIAM EDWARD PHILLIPPS didn't want much.

All he wanted was a copy of every single book that had ever been published in the history of the world.

Back in 18th-century England, when the number of books published each year was only a tiny fraction of what gets published today, this idea might not have sounded quite as crazy as it sounds nowadays—but it was close!

Thomas Phillipps was able to start his obsession early because his father was a rich aristocrat who could afford to give his son a big allowance. By 1798, when he was only six years old, Thomas already owned 110 books. That was about 109 more than any of his friends. Most people in those days didn't own any books at all—just a Bible.

By 1811, when he was a student of geography at Oxford University, his library already numbered in the thousands. "You know the extent of your money, and it will be in vain to write to me for more," his father replied when Phillipps wrote home asking for money to buy more books. He pointed out that the year had barely started and Thomas had already spent his entire annual allowance. Why did he need so many books?

Good question.

It might have made more sense if Phillipps had been so fascinated by geography that he was buying hundreds of geography books. But he wasn't. He really didn't care that much about geography. Geography was just an excuse to go to university, which was in London, which was a city full of bookstores, which were places where you could buy hundreds and hundreds of additional—books!!

The fact of the matter was that Thomas Phillipps didn't even care what the books he bought were about.

He was just crazy about books—period. He loved the look of them. He loved the feel of them. He loved their smell, their covers, their papers, their typefaces, their bindings, inks, illustrations, spines, colors, designs. He loved the way books looked on bookshelves—hundreds and hundreds of them, all neatly lined up, floor to ceiling, beautifully printed, bursting with fascinating information.

It was an expensive obsession, even for an aristocrat. Books in the 18th century cost a lot of money because producing a book back then took a huge amount of work. Every page of every book had to be handprinted, and every book handbound. There were no mass-production printing machines in those days. Even an ordinary book cost an equivalent of about $200 today.

By the time Phillipps finished his university education (taking twice as long as everybody else), he was spending about 1,000 pounds per year of his father's money on books—and his father was getting tired of it.

But in 1818, Phillipps's father died, and as the only son, Thomas inherited the family's Middle Hill Estate. This was a huge place, including not only their 21-room mansion but also half a dozen farms covering almost 320 hectares (800 acres). It was mostly the rent from those farms that had been paying the Phillipps's bills. The estate was worth a fortune, but not (as it turned out) to Thomas. After many arguments about Thomas's spending habits, his father had stipulated in his will that his son could only have the rental money from the farms—he couldn't sell the estate itself. Mind you, even the rent money added up to a tidy fortune—almost 7,000 pounds per year. Thomas immediately spent the entire amount on books.

It was about then that he met Henrietta Molyneux, the pretty, outspoken daughter of an Irish major-general. She was his first non-book interest in many years.

Thomas and Henrietta were married in 1819, and for the next two years, during which Henrietta gave birth to two daughters, Phillipps found family life so entertaining and distracting that he only bought about half his usual number of books.

Henrietta approved. She encouraged Thomas to broaden his interests. A hobby was a worthy thing, but when it got out of hand, it could become a problem. They agreed they would take a holiday in Europe for a couple of years and focus on their marriage instead of books.

It was a big mistake.

The 1820s turned out to be the perfect time to buy books in Europe. During the Napoleonic Wars, which had just ended, a great many European libraries had been looted and damaged, and their books were now being sold off. Suddenly, books were plentiful—and cheap. They weren't just being sold singly, or by the bundle, or by the box. They were being sold by the crateful, the wagonful, and the roomful! Phillipps felt like a kid in a candy store.

When Thomas and Henrietta returned to England two years later they brought back a third daughter, a marriage that was in shambles, a staggering debt load, and 56 massive crates full of books.

Phillipps told his friends his holiday had been a great success.

His father-in-law, who'd been looking after Middle Hill for them during their holiday, called on Thomas to have a heart-to-heart talk. Thomas's estate earned a fortune, he pointed out, yet

Middle Hill was going to ruin, Thomas appeared to owe money to every bookseller in England, and some of his servants hadn't received a farthing in two years!

Thomas shrugged. He pointed out that his father's will had put Middle Hill into a trust. If he could sell the estate he'd be able to pay his debts.

"Your father obviously knew you well," Mr. Molyneux said grimly. "If you could sell Middle Hill, you would simply buy books with the proceeds and send your family to the poorhouse!"

Which was true.

By now Middle Hill was so full of books that 16 of its 21 rooms were being used only for book storage. Even the girls' bedrooms were so full that there was barely room for their beds. The master bedroom contained so many books that Henrietta had to get up on her bed to get dressed. The hallways and vestibules had floor-to-ceiling stacks of books packed so close together that people had to walk sideways down the halls to get through.

Even more bizarre, the place was beginning to look alarmingly like a funeral home. Afraid of fire, Phillipps didn't store his books on bookshelves like most people. Instead, he'd gotten a coffin-maker to adapt his cheapest coffin so that its side wall opened downward on hinges. Phillipps stored most of his books in such coffins now—hundreds of coffins stacked one on top of the other in rows. That way they could quickly be hauled out of the house in an emergency.

Visitors to Middle Hill reported other odd features, like the pieces of firewood scattered all over the floors. Phillipps had discovered that Middle Hill was infested with beetles—the kind that liked to eat wood, and if wood wasn't available—books! So he scattered his firewood logs all over the house and checked them regularly. Whenever he saw telltale piles of sawdust beside any log, he knew that a beetle had taken the bait. That log went into the fireplace at the next opportunity.

Every serious book collector needs to keep records of what he owns, and because Phillipps was too cheap to hire cataloging clerks, everyone in the house had to pitch in. One of the first things Phillipps's three daughters learned as soon as they were old enough to start home-schooling was how to read book titles and catalog them. That's how they spent most of each school day, instead of learning math or geography or chemistry.

So did their governess, their tutor, and even their mother!

By 1830 Phillipps owed money to so many people that most local merchants refused to do business with him anymore. He spent hours every day dodging bailiffs, tax collectors, bank investigators, and even the police. Every few months the pressure became so bad that he had to escape to London, so his estate manager could say in all truthfulness that he hadn't seen him and didn't know where he could be found. But every time he came back, he brought back more cratefuls of books.

By this time Phillipps had perfected a number of scams to help him purchase books he couldn't pay for. They weren't very sophisticated, but they worked amazingly well.

1) He borrowed money from everybody and anybody—then used method #2.

2) He ignored all bills until the vendors sued, then fought the suits in court. It was surprising how often he won, or at least was able to reduce the bill.

3) He bought on long-term credit—buy now, pay later—then used method #2.

4) He bought "on approval," then "forgot" to return the merchandise, sometimes for years. If the vendor finally sued, he used method #2.

5) He offered suspicious booksellers higher than usual prices to convince them to sell—then used method #2.

6) He ordered books from foreign booksellers who were unaware of his payment record—then used method #2.

7) He bought up the entire stock of bankrupt booksellers at distress prices—often booksellers who'd gone bankrupt because of Phillipps's refusal to pay! Then he used method #2.

In short, when it came to acquiring books, Thomas Phillipps was a heartless scam artist. He knowingly and continually bought far more books than he could possibly pay for, not caring whose life he destroyed and whose business he ruined.

In fact, the only reason merchants still sold Phillipps anything at all was because they knew he earned 7,000 pounds of estate rent each year. They reasoned that even if he spent more than that, this amount at least would be paid down annually on his debts—and who knew? They might be one of the lucky ones to be paid!

Phillipps was quite happy to use such desperation to keep his scams going year after year.

As Phillipps's obsession grew worse, so did his behavior. He became crankier and more ruthless. He even cheated a printer he'd hired to print his catalogs. When the man complained that the barn he was working in was a ruin, and his machinery and papers were being destroyed by rain, Phillipps told him to count his blessings that he had a job at all.

"Employment without payment is no blessing," the printer replied.

Phillipps didn't treat his own family much better. Henrietta tried everything she could think of to patch up their marriage. She begged Thomas to write her a letter once in a while when he was in London. Even a short note would do. Something to let her know what he was doing, how he had spent his day.

Phillipps replied impatiently that there was nothing what-soever to tell. He got up in the morning, spent the day buying books, then went to bed. That was all the news there was.

Henrietta felt increasingly abandoned and began to feel de-pressed. In the fall of 1831 her bouts of depression became worse. She began to take opium, a common anti-depressant of the time. Phillipps didn't even notice.

She died alone in February of the following year, while Phil-lipps was in London. She had sent a message to his lodging house to tell him she was very sick, but he'd ignored it. Even after he received the message of her death, he didn't come home for another four days.

Phillipps wasted no time in searching for a new wife—prefer-ably a very rich one so he could pay off his debts and buy more books.

"I'm for sale for 50,000 pounds," he wrote to a friend. "Do you know of any lady with that amount of income?"

His friend didn't, so Phillipps got to work. Over the next few months he wrote to the parents of 17 rich heiresses. "I've been given to understand that your daughter will inherit a substantial estate. I am writing to ask if this is true, and what the value of the estate will be. If the amount is large enough, I intend to ask for her hand in marriage."

His letters were so frankly business-like and unsentimental that one father angrily accused him of acting like a cattle dealer!

Another friend put it a little more diplomatically. "My dear Thomas," he cautioned. "Women are not books."

Phillipps was rejected by all 17 families.

The only people Phillipps seemed genuinely to like were scholars. With scholars he was helpful, considerate, even generous.

As his library grew, more and more scholars asked permission to come to Middle Hill to use it. They were always welcomed—both by Phillipps *and* by his daughters. It was the girls' only chance to enjoy some company, as their father didn't approve of girls going to parties or dances.

Phillipps probably didn't want his daughters to go to parties because he was afraid they would meet young men and get married. They were far more valuable to him as free labor. By 1841, all three were working for him full-time as librarians in his enormous library.

But on February 22, 1842, Middle Hill received a visitor whose effect on the entire Phillipps family over the next 30 years would be profound.

His name was James Orchard Halliwell, and he was a Shakespeare scholar. He was as obsessive about books and documents dealing with Shakespeare as Phillipps was about books in general.

Halliwell's eyes nearly popped out when he saw Phillipps's many rare and valuable Shakespeare documents. The two men got along very well because Phillipps liked anybody who liked books that much.

But then Halliwell became almost as fascinated with Phillipps's eldest daughter Henrietta as he was with Phillipps's books. Phillipps became suspicious, and then alarmed. He began making anxious inquiries about Halliwell's background.

At first he was told that Halliwell was a brilliant young scholar whose impulsive purchases of Shakespeare documents had sometimes gotten him into financial trouble. (Phillipps had no trouble understanding that.) But Halliwell didn't have a rich family to bail him out, so he had turned a number of friends into enemies by failing to repay loans. (Still no reason for Phillipps to become alarmed.) Then Phillipps made a discovery that genuinely horrified him. Several years earlier, James Halliwell had been caught by the British Museum stealing rare and precious manuscripts, which he had tried to sell to pay off his debts.

He was a book thief!

Phillipps immediately banned Halliwell from Middle Hill. But it was already too late. Henrietta had fallen in love with her admirer. And when the two eloped six months later, Phillipps discovered that a rare edition of *Hamlet* was missing from his Shakespeare collection.

Phillipps was talking with his lawyer about the possibility of having Halliwell arrested for book theft when his lawyer alerted him to a much bigger problem: that since Halliwell had married Phillipps's eldest daughter, he would eventually inherit Middle Hill. Even worse, if something wasn't done to protect Phillipps's library, Halliwell would inherit that too—which had no doubt been a part of the young man's plans all along.

"There is nothing you can do about Middle Hill," the lawyer explained quickly, when he saw the shock on Phillipps's face. "It must be passed on to your eldest child, like it or not. But your book collection is another matter. You can give that to anyone you please. Just make certain that your will includes explicit instructions to keep Halliwell away from it."

"You can rely on that," Phillipps scowled. "I'll make very certain of that. But let's return to Middle Hill. I understand that I can't dispose of it, or deed it to someone else—it must be passed on to Henrietta. But does it matter what condition it's in when she receives it?"

His lawyer looked puzzled. "Its condition? No, I don't believe the will says anything about its condition. Why? What do you have in mind?"

Phillipps laughed, but there was no humor in his voice. "You'll see," he said grimly. "Just give me a little time and you'll see."

Around the time of his daughter's elopement, the 50-year-old Phillipps had married again. Her name was Elizabeth Mansel, she was 27 years old, and she wasn't rich—her father was a church minister. But she was astonishingly patient, and a good thing too. More boxes and crates of books arrived every day, and Mary and Katharine, the two daughters still living at home, did their best to update the records.

Thomas Phillipps's debts increased, and the living space for Middle Hill's residents shrank more and more. Then, not long after their wedding, Phillipps began to follow through on the threat he'd made in his lawyer's office.

The first sign of what Phillipps had in mind was the arrival of a small army of timber cutters. They began to cut down the dozens of majestic oaks and elms and ash trees lining the long, beautiful drive through the Middle Hill estate to the mansion's front door.

Then they began to chop down the forest around the mansion itself.

Horrified, James Halliwell appealed to the Courts for a restraining order. There had to be some way to stop this reckless destruction of his future inheritance! The judge saw his point, but said his hands were tied. The will that protected the ownership of Middle Hill didn't say anything about its condition.

There was nothing Halliwell could do but watch in despair as Phillipps systematically destroyed the Middle Hill estate.

"He's cut down every tree and ornamental bush," Halliwell reported to Henrietta, who refused to watch the carnage. "He's ripped up the gardens and destroyed the ponds. He's even let in cattle to ruin the lawns and trample the nurseries and the flowerbeds!"

And that was only the beginning of what Phillipps intended. With the money he received for the Middle Hill timber, Phillipps eventually bought himself a mansion more than twice the size. It was called Thirlestaine House, and was located near Cheltenham, about a day's journey north. And on April 27, 1863, Phillipps called in the movers.

Moving the family's possessions to Thirlestaine House took only three days, using a single cart, one horse, and one driver.

Moving Phillipps's library took a fleet of more than 100 wagons, 230 cart horses, and 175 men an astounding eight months, working dawn till dusk, six days a week! The wagons were often so overloaded that many of them suffered broken wheels and axles, which remained scattered along that stretch of road for years afterwards. Even after eight months the drivers had only transferred about three-quarters of Phillipps's library, but they rebelled and stopped work when Phillipps once again became hopelessly behind in his payments.

Thirlestaine House was so huge and its corridors so long that Phillipps actually rode a horse through them to get from one wing to the other while his books were being brought in. Its kitchen was almost a city block away from its dining room—by the time the food arrived for dinner, it was always cold. Elizabeth hated the house from the start.

But it was a great place to store books—hundreds of thousands of books. By now Phillipps had become so insane for them that when a bookseller sent him a catalog, he often just ordered everything it listed. If he entered a bookshop, he often bought its entire contents. If at all possible, he preferred buying entire libraries, complete auction book lots, and whole warehouses full of books.

He even took to buying wagonloads of wastepaper on its way to the dump—just in case they contained valuable documents, manuscripts, or books.

When his entire library had finally been transferred to Thirlestaine House three years later, Thomas Phillipps turned his attention back to his further plans for Middle Hill.

If James Halliwell thought he had seen the end of its destruction, he was in for an ugly surprise.

Phillipps now proceeded to strip the house of every nut and bolt and fitting that could be removed. He tore off the gutters and smashed down the chimneys. He removed every cabinet, door, and window casing. He allowed vagrants to move in, and vandals to smash whatever he hadn't removed.

Middle Hill was reduced to a complete ruin.

After decades of tyranny, Phillipps's remaining daughters quickly found themselves husbands and fled. At this point even the ever patient Elizabeth found life with Thomas Phillipps too much to handle. "Books, books, books!" she cried. "Your books are going to be the ruination of you, Thomas Phillipps!" Not long afterwards she had a mental breakdown and was sent off to live in a cheap boardinghouse in southern England.

Phillipps mailed her a little money now and then, but never enough to pay her rent. When her family wrote him to protest the way he was treating their daughter, Phillipps replied: "Well, why don't *you* take care of her? You have some money—I don't. All I have is debts."

During the last four years of his life, Thomas Phillipps turned into a total hermit. Most of his servants left him, and he stopped receiving visitors. He hardly seemed to eat or sleep anymore. He just roamed around his house day and night, unwrapping, shelving, and cataloging more books. If a servant found him asleep, it was usually in the middle of the floor or at some table, surrounded by great piles of books.

Thomas Phillipps died on February 6, 1872—several days after falling from a ladder he'd been using to reach some books stored high up near the library ceiling.

In his will, he left his spectacular collection—by now the largest privately held library in the world—to Thomas Fitzroy Fenwick, the baby son of his youngest daughter Katharine, in the desperate hope that the boy would grow up to love books as much as his grandfather. In the meantime, he specified that the book thief James Halliwell, inheritor of Middle Hill, was never to be allowed into Thirlestaine House, and certainly nowhere near Phillipps's treasured books.

To his wife Elizabeth, as "a token of his affection," he left the miserable sum of 100 pounds.

Whether or not Thomas Phillipps's final hope—that his grandson would love books as much as he had—came true depends on your definition of the word "love."

According to some people, Thomas Fitzroy Fenwick turned out to be even *worse* than his Uncle James Halliwell, the book thief. While his grandfather Phillipps had spent his entire life *collecting* books, Thomas Fenwick spent his entire life *selling* the books his grandfather had collected.

But he didn't just dump them. He didn't just take the money and run. No, he spent his entire life patiently evaluating and documenting his grandfather's books, while carrying on the world's longest, slowest, and most carefully conducted library book sale ever.

It made him and his family very wealthy, but it also meant

that none of the wealth was wasted. Thomas Fenwick "harvested" his inherited book collection so carefully that when he died and the library passed into the hands of *his* eldest son, only a small fraction of it had actually been sold.

This process has now gone on for over 130 years, and continues to the present day. Although the library has since passed out of the hands of Phillipps's descendants, its sale has gone on in the same careful way. Known as the Bibliotheca Phillippica, its books continue to be listed for sale on the Internet and in antiquarian auctions all over the world.

And if the current owners maintain this same wise and patient approach, the proceeds from Bibliotheca Phillippica may very well enable many more generations of book lovers to benefit from the manic obsession of the world's most ruthless and devious book collector.

La Grande Thérèse Steps Out

THÉRÈSE D'AURIGNAC WAS HAVING A LOT OF TROUBLE getting used to being a servant girl.

People ordered you around like you were dirt. They worked you like an ox. They treated you like a slave. Men made unfeeling and indecent passes at you.

Thérèse's family had always been poor—in fact, her father had been no more than a peasant in her home village of Bauzelles, France—but at home she'd always been treated like the intelligent, resourceful girl she was.

That had all changed two years ago on January 5, 1874, when her father, René D'Aurignac, had died, leaving the family penniless. This had forced the whole family—Thérèse, her sister, her two brothers, and even her mother—to become servants to rich families in the nearby city of Toulouse. If you had no money in 19th-century France, going into service was usually your only option. It paid almost nothing, but at least you were fed and given a place to sleep.

Still, this wasn't supposed to have happened. Her father had always promised his family that on the day of his death, they would inherit a large estate.

Thérèse still felt stupid for having believed it—but when you're told the same thing day after day for 16 years, it's hard not to believe it a little bit. Her father's story was that he had actually been born into a very rich family—an aristocratic family—but his rebellious behavior as a young man had gotten him kicked out and disinherited. However, his parents had promised that if he married and made good, his children would be welcomed back into the D'Aurignac family after his death—with fully restored inheritance rights. All the documents proving his story and his family's promise were locked in an old oak chest in his bedroom.

After René D'Aurignac's funeral, the family had gathered in his bedroom to watch Thérèse's brothers Emile and Romain open the chest. Thérèse was pretty sure that nobody else in her family had really believed her father's story either, but now, huddled together and desperate, they all shared the irrational hope that, by some miracle, it might be true anyway.

The lock on the chest was badly rusted. Romain went outside and came back with an axe and a hammer to smash it off.

Inside, they found nothing more than an ordinary brick.

Since then, Thérèse had felt totally cornered. There didn't seem to be any hope. She wasn't a ravishing beauty, so chances of marrying her way out of her situation were just about zero. She was very strong-willed, refusing to be pushed around, so chances of promotion in her work weren't great—in fact, she'd already been fired from almost as many jobs as her father!

The problem, as far as Thérèse could see, was France's class system. It seemed to be completely based on money. If you had money, all doors were open to you. It didn't matter if you were a fool or even a criminal. If you were broke, on the other hand, it didn't matter if you were a champion or a genius—the doors remained closed.

That's all Thérèse could see when she imagined her future—a long row of firmly shut doors.

And then, on March 2, 1881, an unbelievable thing happened.

Thérèse was in a third-class rail car on a train to Paris to visit an aunt, when she saw an elderly American tourist in the first-class car fall out of his seat in exactly the way she remembered her Uncle Jean-Pierre falling off his kitchen chair when he'd had a "fit" several years ago.

Ignoring the rule about third-class passengers not being allowed into first-class cars, she rushed through the glass doors and lifted him up, turning him over onto his side and keeping his tongue from blocking his throat exactly as she'd seen the doctor do to her uncle. "This man needs to get to a hospital right away!" she told the porter who came running to help. "Can you get him a carriage when the train stops at the Gare du Nord?"

She kept massaging the man's neck and shielding him from the sun until the carriage arrived at the nearby Hôpital Lariboisière, where she helped two orderlies put him on a stretcher. But as the orderlies lifted the stretcher to carry him away, the man raised an arm to stop them.

"Who are you, mademoiselle?" he asked in awkward French.

"My name is Thérèse D'Aurignac," she replied.

"Mademoiselle D'Aurignac, will you wait for me until I come out again?"

She said she would do so.

She waited for him in the hospital lobby for almost six hours.

Thérèse spent the next three days caring for this man in his luxurious rooms at the Hôtel Grande Métropolitain. She prepared his medicines, fed him soups from the hotel restaurant, and bathed his head and chest with cool water. When he slept she watched his breathing carefully for any sign of further trouble. He was extremely grateful and thanked her often in a heartfelt and genuine way that was a welcome relief after the way her employers treated her.

He told her his name was Robert Crawford. He was an industrialist from Chicago, on business in Paris—business he had fortunately completed several days ago. He'd been doing a little sightseeing to fill the remaining days before his departure for New York, and still hoped to keep to that schedule. Would Mademoiselle D'Aurignac be willing to help him recuperate until his departure?

He was so charming, considerate and appreciative that she agreed.

Two days later at Le Havre, Thérèse helped him up the gangplank to his steamer—he was still a little shaky—and then bade him goodbye. He kissed her gallantly on both cheeks, pressed her hands with great affection, and then insisted on pushing an envelope into them. He shook his head firmly when she protested.

"You've been absolutely wonderful," he said. "An angel of mercy and generosity. I will never be able to thank you enough."

She didn't open the envelope until she was back on the train to Toulouse.

It contained an amazing 250,000 francs—more money than she had earned in the past two years of domestic service.

In fact, it was enough money to enable Thérèse to free her mother from her servant's job and set her up in her own linen shop.

But this miracle wasn't over. Two years later Thérèse announced that she had received a letter from Sauvignon and Hébert, a legal firm in Paris, informing her that she'd been named in the will of the recently deceased Chicago industrialist Robert Henry Crawford. The will bequeathed to her the astonishing sum of 100 million francs' worth of investments—on two rather unusual conditions:

1) that the inheritance be held in trust at the offices of Sauvignon and Hébert for Thérèse D'Aurignac until she had reached the age of 30;

2) that the inheritance be given to Thérèse D'Aurignac, with accrued interest, on her 30th birthday—but only if or when Thérèse D'Aurignac was married.

It didn't take very long for news of this extraordinary inheritance and its conditions to spread throughout Toulouse.

The most immediate result was that, within days, Thérèse was the most popular girl in town.

Suddenly the young men of Toulouse didn't seem to care that Thérèse was plain-looking, or that her father had been a peasant, or that she was only a domestic servant. Suddenly they all seemed to think that she was beautiful, smart, funny, and ever so charming! It wasn't long before she was receiving lots of marriage proposals.

Doors were beginning to open.

A lot of young women might have let this go to their heads, but not Thérèse. She wasn't fooled. She knew that many of these young men were just interested in her newfound riches. At the same time, she certainly wasn't going to waste the opportunity. She took her time, refused to be rushed, and about a year later chose Frederic Humbert, a lawyer and the son of Toulouse's influential mayor, Gustave Humbert.

It turned out to be a smart choice, because Frederic wasn't at all like Thérèse. She was strong-willed, aggressive, organized, and ambitious. Frederic was quiet, flexible, thoughtful, and a bit scatterbrained. He'd only become a lawyer to please his father. Whenever he could, he withdrew into his studio to paint.

In 1870s France, this was the opposite of the norm. The husband was expected to be the ruler of the family. The wife was expected to be seen but not heard.

But Frederic was perfectly happy to let Thérèse take over the driver's seat. He liked having a strong and decisive wife.

As soon as they were married, the young Humberts moved to Paris. In those days, anybody who was somebody lived in Paris. Paris was at the height of its glory—the capital not only of France, but effectively the whole of continental Europe. Emperor Napoleon III had just spent almost 20 years cleaning and modernizing the city, and it gleamed with new or rebuilt palaces, bridges, monuments, and grand boulevards. It was where the most famous financiers, architects, doctors, and artists of Europe gathered. A fifth of France's entire population lived in Paris.

At first the Humberts moved into a modest townhouse, but that was just temporary. Thérèse had big plans, and it wasn't long before she was putting them into action.

Word of her amazing inheritance had, of course, reached Paris as well—energetically helped along by Thérèse's father-in-law, Gustave. Gustave Humbert had taken a liking to Thérèse as soon as he realized that she was the "son" he'd always wanted! If Frederic had been a disappointment to him, the ambitious and strong-minded Thérèse was a good replacement. The two quickly teamed up on all kinds of projects.

It wasn't long before one Paris banker after another rang Thérèse's doorbell to offer his "services." "Services" was banker talk for "loans." Anyone expecting an inheritance of 100 million francs was a pretty good credit risk from a banker's point of view. The financial community of Paris was telling Thérèse Humbert that she could borrow all the money she wanted.

More open doors.

So that's what Thérèse did. She borrowed money. Tons of money. The first thing she did with it was rescue the rest of her family from their drudge-jobs. Then she bought a huge mansion on the fashionable Avenue de la Grand Armée and had it totally renovated—installing expensive silks, hardwoods, a huge glass solarium with a pool, and a three-story glass rotunda out front. She increased the size of the stables and added a bowling green. She made it the sort of place that politicians and financiers and socialites would be impressed by. (Frederic, on the other hand, just had the carpenters add a modest painter's studio to the rear of the mansion, where he spent most of his time contentedly practicing his watercolor techniques.)

When the mansion was ready, Thérèse turned her attention to country estates. Everyone who was someone in Paris had a country estate. She bought two—one in Provence, another in Avignon—and a classy yacht that she moored in Le Havre. Meanwhile she filled her closets with clothes and jewelry.

By 1885, at the age of 27, Thérèse Humbert was well on her way to becoming an important person in Paris. Her salon was one of the most interesting meeting places in the city, attracting all kinds of fascinating people—painters, politicians, writers, lawyers, and businessmen.

This was all the more surprising since Thérèse herself had not had a rich girl's education. She had never learned how to be elegant and witty. She was plain-spoken, and hard-headed in her opinions. She had a scratchy voice and a bit of a lisp. But people liked the way she didn't try to put on airs. They liked her sense of humor and her genuine curiosity. She learned quickly, and had an instinctual sense for how to dress, how to mingle, and how to put people at ease. She soon acquired a reputation for being lively and thought-provoking—and for treating her servants decently.

Once Thérèse had assembled all the basic requirements for a life of influence in Paris, she began tackling the world of business. She'd always wanted to be a businesswoman, and with her wealth this was now a realistic possibility. She teamed up with her two brothers, Emile and Romain, and began by investing in real estate. She bought houses, estates, office buildings, and warehouses. Then she consulted Frederic about art and bought paintings: El Grecos, Velazquezes, Daumiers, and Toulouse-Lautrecs. She also invested in a number of art galleries (whose owners, if they knew what was good for them, quickly developed an enthusiasm for Frederic's watercolors).

She drove hard bargains and kept a sharp eye on expenses. Her investments made money. She used some of it to pay down her debt, but she also gave generously to charities and cultural projects recommended by her father-in-law. That raised her profile among Paris' politicians and social leaders. Gustave Humbert was teaching her well.

Fewer and fewer of that long row of doors remained closed.

Then, in 1886, there was a shocking development. A front-page story in the French newspaper *Le Matin* announced that a challenge had been filed in U.S. Supreme Court against the last will and testament of Robert Henry Crawford.

The challengers were said to be two nephews of Thérèse's benefactor—named Robert and Henry Crawford. The nephews claimed to have found another will—undated—which listed *three* beneficiaries of their uncle's estate: Thérèse D'Aurignac, Robert Crawford, and Henry Crawford.

They were thus challenging the right of Thérèse Humbert to receive the entire Crawford estate when she turned 30—the inheritance that had convinced the bankers of Paris to lend Thérèse every penny she'd used to buy her properties and businesses!

For a few days, the bankers were quite alarmed. But then word got around that Gustave Humbert—who had recently been named France's Minister of Justice—had examined the documents and had decided that Thérèse had a very strong case. Everybody calmed down again.

Thérèse's own reaction, of course, was typical Thérèse. She was furious. There was no way she was going to let herself get pushed around by these upstart Crawford nephews. She marched down to the offices of Sauvignon and Hébert and demanded to be given those inheritance documents. When Monsieur Sauvignon objected that according to the will, she wasn't supposed to be given the documents until she was 30, she said she only wanted to store them in a place where she'd know for certain those Crawford nephews couldn't get their fingers on them—a safe in her own bedroom! She said she was prepared to sign a guarantee that the safe would not be opened, and the documents would not be touched by anyone, until the courts determined the rightful owner. Somehow, she managed to talk Monsieur Sauvignon into agreeing to this arrangement.

That safe in Thérèse's bedroom became famous throughout the French financial community—especially among the bankers of Paris. It contained the inheritance against which they had loaned her, by now, over 70 million francs. They were as anxious to keep those documents out of the hands of the Crawford nephews as she was.

To make sure this remained so, Thérèse announced that she had hired a small army of American lawyers to challenge the nephews' claim. The nephews, apparently, did the same to challenge hers.

The case began to grind its way slowly through the American courts.

While all this was going on, Thérèse kept expanding her business empire. One of her biggest projects during this time was the founding of an insurance company with her brothers Emile and Romain. Known as the Rente Viagère, this company sold life insurance, and like Thérèse's other companies, it received very positive newspaper coverage. (Being the daughter-in-law of the country's Justice Minister always helped to attract positive newspaper coverage.) Within a fairly short time it too was reported to be making a tidy profit.

No matter what sort of business she undertook, "La Grande Thérèse," as she came to be called, couldn't seem to fail.

She was doing well on the social and political front too. Her circle of influential friends was growing steadily. She'd managed to talk Frederic into running for Parliament, and he'd won a seat. There was talk of her father-in-law becoming Leader of the Senate. The President of France himself had come to the Humbert mansion for dinner on several occasions.

Then, in 1888, Thérèse Humbert turned 30—the age at which her inheritance from Robert Henry Crawford should have been handed over to her. But the court case in the United States was still dragging on, showing no signs of being settled. So everyone shrugged and just kept waiting. After all, Thérèse was paying the interest on her loans without fail, and making French bankers a lot of money. There was no point in trying to fix something that wasn't broken.

Which wasn't to say that there weren't any complainers at all. Monsieur Jules Bizat, for instance. This short, dumpy little man worked as an investigator for the Bank of France, so being suspicious was part of his job. One day, while talking to a banker named Monsieur Delatte, the two men discovered they'd both been wondering about some of Thérèse Humbert's stories. Hadn't anyone found it strange that her court case with the Crawford nephews had been going on for over two years now, with no resolution in sight?

"Well, you're going to New York in a few weeks, aren't you?" Bizat said. "Why don't you look those Crawfords up and get their side of the story?"

Delatte agreed. The next time he ran into Thérèse Humbert, he asked her casually where these remarkably quarrelsome Crawford nephews lived.

Thérèse said they lived in a suburb of Boston.

During his trip to America, Delatte made a side trip to Boston. He searched the city's property records and even its voting records for a Robert or Henry Crawford. No luck. He then tried Chicago, the hometown of Robert Henry Crawford. No luck there, either.

Delatte telegraphed this information back to Bizat.

Bizat made an appointment at Thérèse's office and confronted her with Delatte's information. Thérèse just laughed.

"I didn't mean Boston, Massachusetts," she said. "I meant Boston, Georgia. The Crawfords have lived in Georgia for over a hundred years."

Bizat felt like a fool.

But when he tried to contact Delatte back in New York to ask him to check out Thérèse's explanation, he was informed that Delatte had been mugged several days earlier and had died in a New York hospital. It was pure coincidence, and had nothing to do with his investigations into Thérèse Humbert's court case, but the result was that Bizat's own investigations fizzled.

Thérèse Humbert's position in Paris society remained secure.

It wasn't until early 1901 that a muckraking journalist, Emile Zola—who was also a famous novelist—began writing accusing articles in *Le Matin* about Thérèse Humbert and her companies. He questioned why nobody seemed curious about the Crawford nephews' court case that had been dragging on, by this time, for over 15 years. He also wondered why no one had ever checked Madame Humbert's famous bedroom safe to verify that it indeed contained an inheritance worth 100 million francs.

Most people reading *Le Matin* just grinned at Emile Zola's jabs. Zola was famous for making wild and unproven accusations. Even Thérèse Humbert just shrugged and ignored him.

But her chief attorney, Maître du Bruit, took Zola's comments personally.

Without consulting Thérèse, he wrote a furious letter to *Le Matin,* accusing Zola of slander. He said that Zola had done irreparable damage to his honor. He threatened mayhem and prosecution. If Zola was suggesting there was something suspicious about the Crawford will, well, he could prove otherwise. Madame Humbert had nothing to hide. Indeed, he was prepared to open Madame Humbert's safe and to let *Le Matin* or anyone else examine the documents in question if they thought it was so important. That would settle the issue!

When Thérèse was informed of du Bruit's letter, she was appalled.

She asked du Bruit what on earth he was doing. She reminded him that she'd signed an assurance with Sauvignon and Hebert that no one would open that safe or handle its documents until the courts had ruled on the rightful owner.

Du Bruit hadn't forgotten that. But it wasn't a problem, he assured Thérèse. There was an article in French inheritance law that allowed for the opening of officially sealed documents if it was in the public interest. He was quite sure he could invoke that law in this particular case. After all, not just his honor had been challenged by Zola, but hers, too.

Thérèse snapped that she didn't give a fig about her honor! What she was afraid of was that opening the safe would jeopardize the Crawford court case in the United States—just when it seemed to be coming to a conclusion!

At this, du Bruit became huffy. He said he had seen no evidence that the Crawford case was coming to a conclusion. If it was, he certainly hadn't been informed about it.

Thérèse Humbert threw up her hands and charged out of the room.

But when she turned to her various legal and political friends for help to block du Bruit from opening her safe, Thérèse found herself running into unexpected resistance. Zola's articles had been more effective than she'd expected. The prime minister himself, it was whispered, had now "taken an interest" in her case. He was said to be of the opinion that the only sensible way to resolve this issue was to open the safe.

A prime minister's "opinion" in France in the early 1900s had a lot of clout.

Two days later, a mysterious fire broke out in the Humbert mansion. It burned down a large part of the building's west wing, which was the wing that included Thérèse's bedroom. The bedroom was completely destroyed, but according to the firemen, the safe was a fireproof model. They felt there was a good chance that its contents hadn't been damaged. The only way to make sure of that, however, would be to open the safe and find out.

The fire had given Thérèse such a case of jangled nerves that she packed her bags and told her staff she was leaving for one of her country estates. She told du Bruit that she was dead set against him opening the safe, and if he wanted to go against her express wishes and defy her express orders, she wanted nothing more to do with the matter.

The following week, on May 9, 1901, du Bruit, armed with a court order and surrounded by a crowd of bankers, reporters, and lawyers, instructed several workmen to open the scorched and peeling safe. Since Thérèse had forgotten to leave behind her keys, the workmen had to attack it with hammers and crowbars.

The safe was so massive and indestructible, it took several hours of pounding and smashing before the workmen were able to force open the door.

Inside, they found very little. Not a brick, exactly, but not much more than that. The sealed packets of investments looked impressive, but when they were opened, they were found to be worth less than 5,000 francs in total. Besides these almost worthless documents they found an empty jewelry case, a copper coin, and a brass button.

Then it was discovered that Thérèse, her husband, and her two brothers had all disappeared. Within an hour, a warrant had been issued for their arrest.

All four were found four months later in a boarding house in Madrid, Spain.

When news of the arrests spread across France, Thérèse Humbert promptly became a folk hero.

She had accomplished what most of France's citizens had fantasized doing at one time or another: sticking it to the banks.

Banks were not popular in 19th-century France. They were seen as heartless, tight-fisted, and greedy. Almost everyone had a story to tell about a confrontation with a bank that had ended in financial grief. The idea that a simple, uneducated servant girl had fooled dozens of them into lending her hundreds of millions of francs, and then had risen to become a leader of Parisian high society for no fewer than 20 years—well, it was just too delicious for words.

But even more, they admired Thérèse's pluck. They admired the way she had confronted her poverty and her lack of a decent job. They approved of the way she had rescued her mother, brothers, and sister. And they loved the way she had overcome her lack of beauty and her unpopularity.

The trial that followed, on August 8, 1903, mostly confirmed what everyone already suspected. Although there must have been a real Robert Henry Crawford, or someone like him (where else would Thérèse have gotten those initial 250,000 francs?), everything after that had been pure invention—cooked up with the help of Emile and Romain. The idea of Crawford's will had been their ingenious way of getting Thérèse married and accepted into Parisian high society. The unusual conditions of the will had enabled her to borrow from France's banks without ever having to produce her inheritance.

The provision about the handover at age 30 had been trickier, because that was a solution that had come with a built-in problem. While it had bought Thérèse five years to secure her social and financial position, it meant that at age 30 the game was up—her scam would be revealed. Her initial hope had probably been to become so financially successful during those years that she wouldn't have needed the backing of the imaginary will.

But that part hadn't worked out. Her investments had been profitable, but not nearly enough to pay back 240 million francs. She'd needed more time, so she invented an imaginary set of Crawford nephews to challenge her imaginary Crawford will. This, in effect, had extended the age 30 deadline almost indefinitely, and given her a second chance to make enough money to rid herself of her debts.

Unfortunately, that hadn't worked either—and the main reason was the huge cost of maintaining her high position in Paris society. Buying and maintaining her estates, her yacht, and her lavish parties had made it impossible for Thérèse to make much real financial headway in the end. There was also some suggestion that she'd been forced to make blackmail payments to a number of lawyers who'd discovered her scam years earlier—perhaps including du Bruit.

It took the jury less than 24 hours to find all the defendants guilty as charged. Their sentences, however, were surprisingly lenient. Emile received only two years in prison, Romain three, and Thérèse and Frederic five. Even at that, the crowd outside the courthouse became very angry when the sentences were announced. They'd been shouting that La Grande Thérèse should be set free, with no prison sentence at all. As the four accused were whisked out of the courthouse by a back door with their coats thrown over their heads, they could still hear the crowd shouting and booing and throwing cobblestones out front.

Some analysts suggested that the judge handed down light sentences to avoid an appeal—an appeal that might well have caused a very explosive scandal. They felt that Thérèse Humbert couldn't possibly have pulled off so complex a scam without a lot of inside help—from crooked politicians, crooked lawyers, and quite probably a crooked father-in-law. No one else, however, was ever charged in "L'Affaire Humbert."

The bankers did lose a lot of money—some as much as 45 million francs. Several banks went broke, and a banker from Lyons even committed suicide.

But one banker from Paris, who had lost almost 4 million francs, became a national hero when he was quoted as saying, good-humoredly: "Oh, I'll get paid back somehow, one of these days. And if I don't, well, at least I've had the privilege of serving a truly gifted woman."

John Keely's Good Vibrations

THE ROCHESTER ROOM at the Fifth Avenue Hotel in New York on February 17, 1874 was crowded with reporters.

Some were scribbling in their notebooks. Some were aiming their cameras at a cluster of strange-looking machines and gadgets bolted onto several platforms in the middle of the room.

Some were just watching the tall man with the heavy mustache and long curly sideburns who was busily describing all this mysterious equipment.

"What I'm going to demonstrate is something I call Etheric Force," John Worrell Keely explained. "It's going to make every other form of power in this world obsolete. It is more powerful than any explosive known to man. Its vapor is lighter than hydrogen and so fine it can penetrate metal. But most amazing of all—this force can be harnessed using nothing more expensive than a small amount of ordinary water!"

A few reporters looked fascinated, but most looked doubtful. John Keely had no reputation as an inventor, and he'd always been rather vague about his engineering credentials. The only reason the newspapers were interested at all was that a very famous scientist, the German astronomer Johannes Kepler, had prophesied a very similar "force" in 1625—and Keely was now claiming that he'd finally found it.

If Keely noticed the reporters' doubts, he gave no sign. He calmly went on to describe the astonishing new Etheric Force engine he was currently developing. He claimed it would require no more than a single liter (quart) of water to drive a 30-car train all the way from New York to San Francisco at a speed of 120 kilometers (75 miles) per hour. Powering a steamship across the Atlantic Ocean from New York to Liverpool would require at most 4 liters (a gallon).

Several reporters snorted, and one jeered openly, saying, "I'll believe that when I see it."

Keely replied that he had already run a 40-horsepower test motor at 800 revolutions per minute for more than 15 uninterrupted days, and it had used less than a thimbleful of water.

He led the group to a platform on which he had mounted a large brass globe filled with a mass of wires, tubes, and disks. He explained that this was a "shifting resonator," which activated the "vibrational energy" in the water. This energy was then passed through a "vibratory liberator-transmitter" (he pointed to a steel casing bristling with variously sized steel rods), which in turn drove his "hydra-pneumatic pulsating-vacuum engine." He indicated a heavy steel drum mounted inside a thick iron hoop.

"Why can't you use ordinary English?" a reporter complained. "This is all such nonsense. I can't understand a word you're saying."

Keely explained that his concept was so new that words hadn't been invented for it yet—so he'd had to make them up himself. He apologized for the difficulty. "But I think you'll have no trouble understanding this," he said. "Please watch carefully."

He picked up a small shot glass of water and poured it slowly into an intake port on the resonator. Then he switched on both the resonator and the transmitter. They hummed quietly.

Keely explained that his transmitter could actually accommodate seven different levels of vibration, and that he'd be able to double or even triple those levels as his research progressed.

Then he picked up a tuning fork and struck it against a piece of metal. A strong, clear hum sounded through the room. Keely held the humming fork close enough to the resonator to almost touch it.

Immediately, the steel rods of the transmitter began releasing a fine haze that looked like water vapor. Seconds later, the needle of a pressure gauge on Keely's engine zoomed from 0 to 23,000 kilograms (50,000 pounds). With a vicious hiss, the motor started to spin, very fast, then violently, its speed increasing to a frightening howl.

Keely pointed meaningfully at a length of thick, steel industrial cable that had been fastened between two enormous iron buckles. Then he threw the lever on a huge hydraulic piston and quickly stepped back.

There was a scary-sounding *twang!!* as the cable became so rigid, it started to vibrate.

Keely ducked, gesturing for everyone to cover their heads.

There was a brief drop in the howl of the motor, and then individual wires of the steel cable began to snap with small, sharp explosions. An instant later the entire cable ruptured with a stunning, teeth-rattling bang, showering everyone with sparks and tiny bits of red-hot cable. A cloud of acrid dust from the disintegrated cable filled the room.

Keely groped his way through the haze and switched off the resonator, and the awful howl of the motor slowly died away.

As the dust cleared, the reporters straightened up and began shaking bits of blackened metal off their clothes. Some had dropped their notebooks and cameras in fright. Many looked shaken.

"And that," Keely said with a satisfied grin, "is merely a very small demonstration of the amazing power of Etheric Force. Good day, gentlemen!"

The headlines in New York's newspapers the next morning were everything Keely could have hoped for.

"Etheric Force Power of Tomorrow," read one. "Astounding Demonstration of Water Power," read another. "Simple Tap Water Will Power Trains, Ships," announced a third. By noon, Keely's message box at the Fifth Avenue Hotel was bulging with telegrams.

All sorts of people wanted to know more about his amazing machine. Newspaper editors who had ignored his invitation. Scientists and engineers who were fascinated or suspicious. Businessmen looking for a hot new investment opportunity. And everybody wanted to see how a few cups of water could drive an entire freight train from New York to San Francisco!

Keely patiently demonstrated his Etheric Force again and again. Sometimes his motor snapped pieces of industrial cable. Sometimes it twisted iron bars into pretzels. Each time his spectators were enormously impressed.

It wasn't long before Keely was meeting with some of the richest businessmen in the United States. Charles B. Franklin, head of the Cunard Steamship Line. Henry S. Sergeant, president of the Ingersoll Rock Drill Company. John J. Cisco, head of the Cisco National Bank. John Jacob Astor, son of the richest man in America. They all assembled at Keely's small machine shop on North Twentieth Street in Philadelphia.

The first thing they wanted to know was whether Keely had taken out a patent on his Etheric Force idea, and whether he would consider teaming up with other inventors in the same field, such as Thomas Edison, who was working on an electric lamp. If Etheric Force could produce electric light, its possibilities were endless!

"Gentlemen, gentlemen," Keely responded. "The answer to both questions is no. I know nothing about business, and I have no interest in learning anything about it. I simply wish to continue my research. To register a patent, or work with other scientists, I would have to share the details of my discovery, and I cannot take that chance. I am not prepared to risk the loss of my years of work—not to mention the potential profits."

His listeners nodded. They had all heard of dishonest inventors stealing other people's scientific discoveries. And they also knew that Keely's discovery could be worth a tremendous amount of money. Machines in the 1870s ran on steam, which was a very dirty form of power. You had to burn a lot of coal or wood to make steam, and that produced a lot of soot and ashes. Everything near a steam engine got coated with soot. Train stations were black with it. When you took a train, your clothes became smeared with it. If you lived near a railroad, the laundry on your clothesline became black with it.

A new form of power that used only water and produced no smoke at all would be a truly fantastic development.

One of the businessmen suggested incorporation. Research was expensive, but with a group of investors backing him, Keely could improve and speed up his research. "I believe I speak for all the gentlemen present when I say that we'd be interested in making an investment in such a company," he said. "Call it, perhaps, the Keely Motor Company."

The Keely Motor Company was duly incorporated on March 15, 1874. Keely's investors, who became the company's directors, paid him an astounding $15 million for half of his company's shares.

For the next three years John Keely worked away busily in his machine shop. No one knew what he was doing in there, because he was a very secretive man and always kept his doors and windows locked. He smeared his windows with white paint and only opened them for ventilation, or to let out the dust and smoke after one of the periodic explosions people in the neighborhood heard coming from the machine shop. Keely never explained the cause of these explosions to anyone.

Every year for the directors' annual meeting, Keely prepared more demonstrations of his mysterious Etheric Force. He made his magical little engine lift big weights and produce amazing pressures. But after three years of these performances the directors began to grow impatient.

They complained that all this crashing and banging and ripping was certainly entertaining, but what they were waiting for was a commercially usable motor. One they could sell to the builders of ships and locomotives, and most especially automobiles, which were very much the coming thing.

Keely assured them that such a motor was precisely what he'd been working on for the past three years, and that he'd be ready to give a public demonstration of it in three months, on July 1. It would power a circular saw, running at 3,500 revolutions per minute. Five drops of water would be used to cut 10 cords of wood.

But on June 29, 1877, John Keely sent his directors a cancellation telegram. REGRET TO INFORM THAT I HAVE ENCOUNTERED PROBLEMS HARMONIZING NEGATIVE AND POSITIVE VIBRATIONS OF MOTOR'S MAIN SHAFT, STOP. MUST POSTPONE DEMONSTRATION TO A FUTURE DATE, STOP. WILL BE IN TOUCH SOON, STOP.

"Negative and positive vibrations—what on earth is that supposed to mean?" a director demanded. None of the others had a clue.

They didn't hear from Keely again for over six months.

When they finally did, it was a note from him to explain that he had abandoned work on his Etheric Force engine because he had discovered a newer, even more powerful and efficient form of energy—something he was calling "Vibratory Sympathy."

The beauty of Vibratory Sympathy, Keely explained, was that it was based on the simple fact that everything on earth vibrates. That was a huge energy source. To tap into it, all you had to do was find the right combination of musical notes to get it started. You didn't need resonators or transmitters. You didn't even need water! So that's what he'd been researching during the past half year.

Now he was working on a motor to harness that energy, and it was almost finished, Keely assured them. He would be demonstrating it in three months' time, on March 1, 1878. It would be startlingly powerful—more than 250 horsepower!

But no one heard from John Keely on March 1, 1878.

They didn't hear from him on March 1, 1879 either—despite several queries and reminders.

On March 1, 1880 the directors of the Keely Motor Company ran out of patience.

They sued Keely in court, demanding that he hand over any of his inventions that might have commercial value, and to force him to explain to an audience of engineers or mechanics just exactly what he had been working on in his machine shop for the past six years.

The suit made headlines throughout the American northeast. "Stockholders Tired of Keely Delays," read one. "Keely Motor Men Disgusted," read another.

In court, Keely admitted that he hadn't yet been able to produce a motor that could be used commercially, but that he was very close. He fully expected to be ready to test his latest prototype—a monster motor that could produce 25,000 horsepower using only vibratory attraction and musical notes as its source of power—by June 1, 1880.

He also agreed to try to explain his newest discoveries to an audience of experts. But he warned the judge that even mechanical specialists might find his ideas hard to understand.

He was certainly right about that. Everyone seemed quite intrigued when Keely activated a small test motor by playing mysterious notes on a violin, but after half an hour of listening to him explaining how this machine "diverted the polar current of apergy quite independent of centrifugal action," most threw up their hands and headed for the door. The few who stayed behind asked to have a closer look at the motor, but Keely absolutely refused to let anyone touch it.

When everyone else had gone, three audience members met at a nearby cafe. One was a professor of physics, John Leidy. The second was a physicist named James Wilcox. The third was a poet named Clara Bloomfield-Moore, the widow of a rich Philadelphia industrialist.

The two physicists were Keely supporters, but his performance had left them worried. Wilcox felt that somehow, whenever he was suspected of being a fraud, Keely managed to behave like one. It tended to make people see everything about him in the worst possible light. And by now he'd spent over $60 million of his investors' money, almost bankrupting the company.

Leidy's view was that Keely was probably a decade or more ahead of his time. After all, the entire universe was made up of energy, and scientists were only just beginning to learn how to use it. But he suspected the Keely Motor Company's directors would never wait that long for results.

"What do you think, Clara?" Leidy asked. "You haven't said a word all night."

Clara took her time answering—and when she did, she looked determined. She said she liked what she'd heard and seen that night. She had no idea what Vibratory Sympathy was all about, but she absolutely loved the idea of a motor that was activated by musical notes.

"I believe I'm going to invest some of my money in the Keely Motor Company," she said.

Reaction in the press to Clara Bloomfield-Moore's astonishing $8 million rescue of the Keely Motor Company was mixed. The *New York Home Journal* praised Bloomfield-Moore for her courageous support of scientific research. *Scientific American* magazine, on the other hand, suggested she was foolishly throwing her money away.

Clarence Moore, Clara's son, agreed with *Scientific American*. He demanded to know what his mother was doing, squandering his inheritance on a crackpot.

Clara pointed out that she wasn't dead yet—and that until she was, how she spent her money was her own business.

Clarence didn't see it that way. He filed a legal suit against his mother, claiming she was a well-meaning but ignorant woman who had fallen under the influence of a scam artist. He lost the suit.

The two didn't speak to each other for the next 15 years.

Clara Bloomfield-Moore became John Keely's most loyal supporter and defender—especially in the press. She wrote enthusiastic articles about him in popular magazines such as *Lippincott's* and the *New York Home Journal*. She hosted elegant parties for him, to introduce him to scientists who might become his supporters, too. She became the only person Keely allowed to wander around his machine shop any time she wanted.

Eventually Bloomfield-Moore wrote an entire book about Keely's work, entitled *Keely and His Discoveries*. Like Keely's lectures, it was so hard to understand that *Scientific American* called it all a bunch of incomprehensible nonsense. John Keely, however, said the lady had gotten it exactly right.

Keely's board of directors really didn't care one way or the other. They just wanted Keely to hurry up and produce that 25,000 horsepower engine! It was now 1887, and they still had absolutely nothing to show for their investment—which had risen to almost $100 million!

It was decided that maybe it was time to take Keely to court again. After all, the only time they'd ever gotten him to cooperate was when they'd used that approach. If they could get the court to order Keely to hand over his test machines, they could hire a real engineer to unpuzzle the technology and build them a commercially salable version.

Hauled into court a second time, Keely was ordered by the judge to comply with his directors' demands. This time Keely refused outright. The judge ordered Keely to be arrested.

When two sheriffs arrived at Keely's machine shop to take him away, they couldn't get in. All the doors and windows were locked. "Open up!" one of them shouted. "Open up in the name of the law!"

There was no answer, but suddenly there was a terrible banging and smashing. Metal crashing into metal. Bursts of glass, and something that sounded like explosions.

"What on earth is going on in there?" a sheriff demanded.

As if in answer, there was another uproar of smashing and banging and bursting. The sharp screech of tearing metal. Thuds and splintering. It went on for at least 10 minutes. Finally the door opened and Keely stepped out.

His hair was hanging into his eyes, his overalls were smeared with oil and soot, and his arms were covered in bleeding scratches. He was carrying a sledgehammer in his fists.

The two sheriffs stepped back abruptly.

"Don't worry—I'm not planning to hurt anyone," Keely said in a tired voice. "You want my machines? Well, you can have them. Take whatever you want."

Inside the shop, it looked as if a bomb had exploded. Everything was smashed to pieces. Cabinets, workbenches, tools, and equipment. Wires, tubes, pipes, and hoses. Shattered glass lay everywhere. And on the floor, in a mangled heap, the remains of Keely's test machines.

The sheriffs called in several men with a cart to haul the mangled machines away. "We think there may have been 11 machines," the sheriffs reported to the judge. "But it could have been as many as 15. There were so many pieces, it was impossible to tell."

Keely spent three days in jail before Clara's lawyers were able to bail him out. During that time he was a model prisoner, quiet and cooperative. The guards liked him.

The engineers, who were hired by the Keely Motor Company couldn't make any sense at all of Keely's machines. They were simply too smashed up to reconstruct.

Faced with the possible loss of their entire $100 million, the directors made a deal with Keely. The inventor promised to rebuild his machines, take out proper patents for them, and then positively and definitely produce a motor for them within five years. In return, the directors agreed to find additional investors to keep the Keely Motor Company afloat for another decade.

Over the next 11 years, after he had rebuilt his machine shop and some of his machinery, Keely began to announce more new and exciting discoveries. He said he had found a way to "vitalize" disks made of a mysterious new metal, which, when charged or "activated" with the proper musical sounds and installed in a special new engine he was building, could produce 250 horsepower of "vibratory thrust" for an entire day on a single charge.

Then he announced he had discovered an astonishing way to use his vitalized disks to enable airships to get off the ground and fly without using huge airbags full of helium gas.

Finally, in 1898, he announced that his "vitalizing" process could be used to fire cannons without using gunpowder. He demonstrated by firing a test cannonball clean through a thick wooden beam, using only a cylinder that had been "vitalized" by the sound of a harmonica. The demonstration impressed both military officials and Keely's directors—especially the new ones who hadn't seen his demonstrations before. The value of Keely Motor Company stock rose for the first time in 15 years.

But he *still* hadn't filed any patents or produced a commercially salable motor.

Clara Bloomfield-Moore was also becoming anxious. She could sense yet another crisis approaching, and this time she suspected things wouldn't go well for John Keely. She suggested once again that he consider forming a partnership with someone trustworthy, to speed up his rate of progress.

"My dear Clara," Keely said patiently, stopping briefly to cough into his handkerchief. "Compared to other great scientific enterprises, my work on vibratory physics is actually progressing at lightning speed!"

That was the last thing John Worrell Keely ever said to his most loyal and enthusiastic supporter. Two weeks later he was dead of pneumonia.

Seemingly within minutes of Keely's death, a riot broke out in front of the Keely Motor Company's offices. Investors, reporters, friends, and enemies rushed into Keely's machine shop, grabbing everything they could get their hands on. Machinery, equipment, papers, models—anything that might contain the secret of Keely's mysterious energy source. For the next several weeks, urgent meetings were held all over the city, as people tried to fit their various parts and pieces together into a working whole—but without success. No one ever found enough of the pieces to assemble an entire model or test machine.

As its directors had feared, the Keely Motor Company was declared bankrupt with no assets to disburse. John Keely had managed to convince dozens of America's most sophisticated investors to give him over a quarter of a billion dollars of their money—without ever producing a single patent or salable product of any kind!

But the story didn't end there. After the affairs of the Keely Motor Company had been wound up, Clarence Moore rented Keely's old machine shop, determined to examine every square inch of it to get to the bottom of Keely's secret.

It wasn't long before he discovered something odd. The floor of the shop had been raised.

There was no question about it. The door to the shop had been shortened, and another step added to the entrance stair.

Moore hurried home to find a crowbar.

Five hours later the shop floor was a wreckage of splintered wood, and Moore was hot on the trail of Keely's 24-year secret.

What he found between the false and the original floor was a network of heavy-duty pipes and valves. The pipes led into a wall and down to the basement, where Moore found the other part of the equation: a huge steel globe buried deep in the dirt. It weighed more than 3,000 kilograms (3 tons) and was obviously a pressure tank, fitted with connections for a compressor.

So that was the force that had driven Keely's mysterious-looking motors: nothing more complicated than cleverly camouflaged compressed air! It was a technology as old and well-known as steam power, and certainly no improvement over it. Yes, it could generate a huge amount of energy, but you still had to burn wood or coal to produce it. To use it, Keely had hidden spring valves under the floor, so he could start his motors by pressing his foot down on a particular spot. The violin had just been a method of distracting attention away from his foot!

So Keely's scam was exposed, and the suspicions of *Scientific American* magazine, which had at various times suggested that compressed air might be behind Keely's clever demonstrations, were confirmed.

But after the uproar had died down, some people began to have further suspicions. Was it possible that Keely's scam had simply been a cover for his *real* research?

Think about it. Everyone agreed that Keely had spent "day and night" in his machine shop. Could it really have taken him 24 years of day-and-night work to build a few fake test motors that operated on nothing more complicated than compressed air?

Not very likely.

Then what had he been doing in there all the rest of the time?

If you do an Internet search on John Keely, you'll discover that Keely's claims for Etheric Force and Vibratory Sympathy haven't gone away. In fact, his ideas seem to be more popular now than they were in his own day.

Some people suggest that Keely simply cooked up his fake demonstrations to attract enough investment money to pay for the research he was *really* interested in—research into a form of energy so bizarre and futuristic that he couldn't possibly have hoped to master it in his own lifetime.

If so, maybe there's still a chance we'll see a motor powered by vibratory sympathy in ours.

Could be. It's not impossible.

And this time, maybe it will be real.

The Imaginary Travels of Karl May

IT WAS 1870 and the 28-year-old German ex–teaching assistant Karl May had just finished reading *The Deerslayer,* by the American novelist James Fenimore Cooper. It was the story of Natty Bumppo, a white boy brought up by Delaware Indians in the American wilderness. Europeans, many of whom lived in squalor in crowded cities with open sewers and few trees—not to mention policemen who enforced an awful lot of rules and regulations—absolutely loved stories about wild Indians roaming the endless forests of America.

So did Karl. Having grown up in a family of 14 children in a crowded tenement, with so little to eat that 9 of his brothers and sisters had died, he had always thrilled to the idea of the wild west of America. Lots of food. Lots of land. Freedom. Adventure!

A bell clanged loudly and a prison guard slammed the door to Karl's cell. "Bedtime, May! Ditch the book! Now!"

Karl sighed and blew out his candle.

It was hard to stop fantasizing an adventure in the American wilderness when you were doing time in a German prison for theft, fraud, and impersonating a medical doctor.

The past 28 years of Karl May's life hadn't exactly been a raving success.

May was smart and ambitious, but he couldn't seem to stay out of trouble. At first it had just been stupid things. He'd been kicked out of teacher's college for stealing a fistful of candles. Then he'd lost his job as a teacher's assistant for making a pass at a married woman.

Then he'd stolen a watch.

The business with the watch had been more serious because that had earned him six weeks behind bars, and in 19th-century Germany a prison record was a serious liability. You couldn't get a decent job once you had a prison record. You couldn't even join the army—May had tried. The only jobs he was able to get involved an exhausting amount of lifting, digging, and hauling.

Pretty soon he was in trouble again. He began swindling people by impersonating officials—pretending to be a university professor, a lawyer, a notary's assistant. One day, dressed as a police officer, he entered a grocery store and ordered the grocer to open his till.

"I'm checking for counterfeit money," he said.

"I'm sure I don't have any," the grocer protested.

"I'll be the judge of that!" May snapped. "Open it up!" He scooped up all the money in the till. "We'll check it down at the police station," he said. "You'll get it back when it's been checked—tomorrow."

He was arrested for that caper two weeks later.

But when he was released, he did it again. He tried impersonating a doctor—and that worked a little better. He started a small medical practice in an outlying German village, but then got carried away and ordered five fitted suits from the local tailor. A doctor, after all, had to keep up appearances! Of course he wasn't able to pay for them, and that led to enquiries. Bingo—another term in prison.

That time, as he was being taken from the court, he somehow managed to undo his chains and escape. But they caught him a year later and now he was serving four years at hard labor. The work involved sawing and splitting firewood 13 hours a day, 6 days a week—but unlike other prisons, this one had a library. Not that there was a lot of time to read—about half an hour a day at most, plus Sunday evenings.

Nevertheless, during the next four years, May managed to read a great many books—most of them adventure and travel stories about wild and exotic places. Several in particular—the novels of James Fenimore Cooper, the travelogues of Friedrich Gerstäcker, and the west Texas travel accounts of the Irish writer Mayne Reid—fascinated May so much that he read them over and over.

As he read them, one thought kept occurring to him again and again: "I bet that I could write stories at least as good as these."

When Karl May was released from prison in 1874, he was 32 years old. He'd spent 8 of the past 12 years in jail, and his prospects for finding a decent job couldn't have been much worse.

But this time he had a plan. The Mayne Reid travel accounts he'd read in prison had given him enough details about the badlands of west Texas to serve as the setting for a story he called "Old Firehand." He now proceeded to write that story. He wrote many drafts of it, trying it this way and that, again and again—crafting and polishing until he was finally convinced that it was really working, that it was the kind of story he himself liked to read.

He was surprised at how much he enjoyed doing it. He was also surprised at how the very act of writing made the adventure come alive in his mind—so alive that it eventually felt as if he'd taken that trip himself. As if he'd really been there.

When May was finally satisfied, he offered the story to the editor of a local publishing company.

"This is very good," the editor said. "Very vivid, very strong. When did you travel in America?"

"Oh... in America? Well... for the past four years," May said hastily.

"Quite the place, I hear," the editor said.

"Oh, it's quite the place, all right," May agreed. "Cowboys. Indians. Buffalo. All those things."

"Our readers like stories like this," the editor said. "Have you got any more like it? If so, bring them to me tomorrow or the next day."

May agreed.

As he walked out of the editor's office, May probably hadn't the slightest inkling that his little lie about traveling to America had just launched him on a scam that would change his life—and that of millions of readers—profoundly.

For the rest of that day, sitting on his filthy little flophouse bunk, May wrote like a man possessed. It was suddenly clear to him that this was his big chance. Perhaps his only chance. Behind him lay a life of embarrassing failures and petty crime. Ahead of him, unless he could make this work, lay a life of drudgery, depression, and probably more time in prison.

But besides the desperation he also felt a burst of exhilaration. He was discovering something he was apparently good at—something he had a knack and an enthusiasm for. And now it seemed he'd found someone who was actually willing to pay him to do this for a living!

No question about it—he simply had to make this work.

May wrote through the entire evening. Then, using candles, he wrote through the entire night. He barely took time out for breakfast, and he completely ignored lunch. By late afternoon he was able to hand the editor a story he called "The Gitano."

The editor was delighted. He bought both stories on the spot, and told May he would buy anything else he'd written along the same lines.

That day Karl May left the flophouse, rented himself an attic that didn't have bedbugs or rats, and bought himself a supply of pencils and paper.

He was in the adventure-story writing business!

It wasn't long before Karl May was making a good living writing stories for a variety of publishers, magazines, and newspapers. He wrote with astonishing speed, and he learned to write whatever his editors wanted: adventure stories, horror stories, war stories, romances. He even cranked out rape-and-murder stories that were known in those days as "penny dreadfuls"—stories in such dubious taste that he wrote them under a pseudonym.

His stories were mostly set in far-off, exotic, or mysterious places: Turkey, Saudi Arabia, Africa, China, Japan, North America, South America. He had never been to any of these places, of course, but he read geography books and history books and travelogues and newspaper accounts—anything that would allow his vivid imagination to fantasize an exotic setting.

He wrote all his adventure stories in the first person, from his own perspective, as if they had actually happened to him. It was what German audiences wanted. True travelogues. The true travels of Karl May, intrepid adventurer. Every hero in his stories had a name that was some variant of "Karl." It made him feel more connected to his stories that way, more directly involved. His publisher never questioned this, and neither did his audience. It didn't seem to occur to him that this might cause him trouble later on in his life.

After half a dozen years of writing stories, May decided to try his hand at novels. That's when his writing career really exploded.

He began with his Winnetou novels, which told the evolving story of a noble Apache chief (Winnetou) who befriends a German traveler (Karl May, alias "Old Shatterhand") and teaches him how to live like an Indian in America's wild West. They become blood brothers, and as their adventures in the Texas badlands multiply in novel after novel, they become an invincible duo, always fighting for the Good and the Right. Between them, they beat the tar out of more villains per page than Superman and Robin!

The Winnetou novels became a smash hit all over Europe, and no wonder. Karl May's timing couldn't have been better. A lot of people in 19th-century Europe had become tired of their leaders' lofty claims about the superiority of their civilization. As far as they could see, all it had ever brought them was endless wars, famines, and disease. So they were fascinated by the idea of the "noble savage"—a person unspoiled by civilization, perhaps primitive, but inherently good, honest, and true. They felt a deep need to return to a kind of world in which goodness triumphed and evil was defeated. So—in sharp contrast to what usually happened when whites and Indians fought each other in American history—in Karl May's novels, the Indians always won. His readers loved that.

By 1890 Karl May was a millionaire, and by 1895 he was the most popular novelist in Europe. His novels were being printed by the hundreds of thousands, and selling in translation as far abroad as Russia and China. He wrote so fast, he often produced two or three novels per year.

It was at this point that May's ego started to run away with him. It had to do with his "autobiographical" adventures. In the beginning, he felt, he hadn't truly lied to his readers about those travels. He'd just written about them from the personal perspective of someone with a name very like his own, and let his readers come to their own conclusions. If they wanted to believe that Karl May really *had* spent years with a noble Apache named Winnetou, outwitting and outgunning dozens of evil outlaws in the badlands of west Texas, that was their business. But now he began to conduct book promotion tours that were cleverly disguised as lectures—lectures about his own "travels" in the wilds of America and the Orient. These lectures proved enormously popular, attracting thousands of enthusiastic fans. They also, of course, sold huge quantities of books.

To give these lectures more credibility, May began dressing in a buckskin jacket and leggings. He strutted around with a rifle slung across his chest and six-guns shoved into his belt. He wore a sombrero or ten-gallon hat, and spurs on his boots. At first he wore these outfits only on his lecture tours, but eventually he took to wearing them in everyday life as well. He began to lace his conversations with words and expressions he claimed were Apache. He chanted "Apache" chants, and took to handing around a peace pipe before his lectures.

He bought himself a large house just outside the city of Dresden, converted it into a hunting lodge, and named it "The Villa Shatterhand." He then hired museum agents in Texas to fill it to bursting with buffalo bones and skulls, American guns, saddles, sombreros, and horseshoes—items he presented as the trophies and mementos of his many journeys to America and elsewhere. His study was crammed with stuffed animals he claimed he'd killed—coyotes, buffalo, mountain sheep, and a huge lion.

In the backyard he had carpenters build an "authentic" log

cabin that he called "Villa Baerenfett" (Villa Bear Fat). He filled this cabin with a fortune's worth of Indian artifacts and jewelry, eagle feathers, dance costumes, peace pipes, and an "authentic" teepee. It was essentially a museum, but was presented as a home away from home for his sidekick, Winnetou.

To journalists who interviewed him, he became unbelievably brazen. He not only *implied* that all this fakery was authentic, he began to insist on it. "Not a single person or event in any of my books is invented," he assured one of them. "Everything is described exactly as I experienced it." He said he could speak over 40 languages, and could understand 120 more. He began to call himself "Doktor" Karl May, implying he had earned a university doctorate—despite the fact that in Europe at this time, a doctorate was so rare and so highly prized that anyone falsely claiming to have earned one could be arrested.

His fans swallowed it all, hook, line, and sinker—but certain tabloid journalists began to have their doubts. Rather than accepting May's version of his life, they began to make enquiries. They tried to track down old friends or colleagues, and looked for family members and relatives.

But they didn't hit pay dirt until somebody discovered that May had been divorced. Once they had tracked down May's ex-wife, Emma, it was game over for Karl May. With Emma's help, it didn't take them long to unearth the whole unsavory truth about May's less-than-heroic former life. German officialdom kept excellent records.

The resulting exposés made headlines all over Europe. "Popular Novelist a Jailbird." "Originator of Winnetou Novels a Liar and a Thief!"

May's fans were stunned, and many were appalled and outraged. His book sales dropped like a rock.

But there was worse to come. In their investigations, the journalists also discovered those lurid penny dreadfuls that May had produced under a pseudonym in his early writing days. Now they had a thief and a liar who also wrote disgusting stories about rape and murder.

It didn't help that May's old publisher promptly decided to take advantage of all this uproar by reprinting thousands of copies of these books—but this time with May's real name prominently emblazoned on the covers!

It all came down on Karl May's head like a ton of bricks.

If the muckrakers had been content to end their attack at this point, May's writing career would probably have come to a crashing halt. But they didn't stop. Their attacks became a real hate campaign. May was accused of being a "sexual pervert" and a "corrupter of youth."

Those were devastating accusations even by European tabloid standards. May counterattacked by suing his old publisher, the newspaper owners, and every one of their journalists for libel. They were court cases he would end up pursuing for the rest of his life.

In the end, May's tormentors went too far and the public began to feel sorry for him. Yes, he'd made some mistakes in his youth, there was no doubt about that. His travel claims and lectures had been untrue, and his books weren't autobiographical at all. But the rest of the accusations against him really seemed over the top. The tabloid journalists had worked themselves into such a frenzy that one journalist even claimed the youthful May had earned his living as a highway robber, hiding out in the woods and attacking passersby with a meat ax!

And besides—when all was said and done, May's books were still exciting to read. Even if they had turned out to be pure fiction.

Public sentiment began to turn against the muckrakers and to side with May. Increasingly, his public forgave him.

His book sales started picking up again.

Wisely, May abandoned his fake lecture tours and refocused all his attention on his writing. During the following decade, novels continued to pour out of him at an astonishing rate. By 1908 he had written 75 books, which had been translated into 39 languages.

That year, at the age of 66, May finally took a trip to the United States, the setting for over 30 of his adventure novels. He'd been reluctant to do this before, because when he'd taken a trip to the Orient 10 years earlier, he'd found the people and the landscapes so different from what he'd described in his novels that he was never able to write a novel set there again. In fact, May had been so shocked at how much he'd misunderstood that he'd actually had a week-long mental breakdown in his hotel in Sumatra, and was nearly committed to an insane asylum.

Unfortunately, his trip to America was a similar disaster. Arriving in New York, he started off by visiting a number of Seneca Indian burial sites and spent several days researching Native American history in the American Museum of Natural History. There, he promptly discovered he'd made all sorts of mistakes in his Winnetou novels, too. He'd assumed the west Texas badlands were a sandy desert, like the Sahara. He'd gotten the Apache and the Pueblo Indians all mixed up, and reported them living in the wrong areas. His European readers had never known the difference, of course, and probably didn't care, but the Americans did— which was one reason why Karl May's novels were largely a flop in the United States.

May was apparently so embarrassed at his discovery that he completely abandoned his plan to visit the American West. In fact, to everyone's astonishment he never ventured beyond a 640-kilometer (400-mile) radius of New York, spending most of his time in a hotel overlooking Niagara Falls and several days touring Toronto and Montreal. About as close as he got to an American Indian was the statue of the Seneca chief Sagoyewatha in a Buffalo cemetery.

He escaped back to Germany after only 42 days in North America, having achieved very little in the way of research or exploration. His bags, however, were bulging with more Indian artifacts, which he'd purchased in New York.

May did write a final Winnetou novel after his return, in which an aging Old Shatterhand returns to Texas from Germany and shows America's Indians how to survive the American government's efforts to annihilate them. This advice provoked John Brant-Sero, an Ojibway Indian visiting Germany, to write an open letter to Germany's newspapers, saying he wished to inform Germany's citizens that he, an American Indian, was getting mightily tired of May's fake expertise. He claimed that he'd tried to contact May to discuss this matter in person, and that May had ignored his letters and his requests to visit.

Not long after that, May abandoned settings in the known world entirely. Instead, he began to write mystical science-fiction tales that took place in outer space or on other planets. He'd never been there either, but the chance of anyone discovering his mistakes in *these* settings—at least in his lifetime—was low.

Curiously, although his fans weren't terribly interested, the literary critics who had sneered at his previous adventure novels judged these books to be his very best.

By the time Karl May died two years later, in 1912, he had written an astounding 82 books, with worldwide sales of over 5 million copies. Despite the exposure of his prison record, and the way he'd deceived his readers, he still remained the best-selling novelist in Europe.

Ironically, Karl May's fakery didn't end with his death. Other entrepreneurs took over his legacy and propelled it to even greater heights. Over half a dozen large outdoor theaters in Germany now put on live performances of scenes from May's novels every summer, featuring German cowboys and German Indians on live horses firing six-guns and rifles. Every weekend, thousands of members of several hundred Karl May societies—doctors, secretaries, plumbers, bus drivers, and lawyers—swarm out into Germany's forests to live in imitation Indian villages, dress in fake cowboy and Indian gear, hold imitation powwows, chant imitation Indian chants, and take imitation ceremonial sweat baths.

They take it all quite seriously—it's not a joke. They see it as a way of getting back to nature, to a world that's more pure and simple than their own crowded, pollution-choked daily lives. And many of them save up for years to travel to North America to visit the places Karl May described in his novels.

Even though he's been dead for almost a century, Karl May remains one of the top-selling authors in the whole world. His book sales have now topped the 200 million mark, and are still climbing steadily. Villa Shatterhand remains one of the most popular museums in Germany, welcoming tens of thousands of visitors every year.

As scams go, this is quite unusual. Most scam victims feel betrayed, cheated, or taken advantage of once the deception has been exposed. But obviously, this isn't always the case. The "victims" of Karl May's deception have decided not to be bothered at all by his fakery.

Which begs the rather interesting question: does a scam remain a scam if its victims refuse to *feel* scammed? Hard to say, but at least this much seems clear: a scam, if it's entertaining enough, can be enjoyed by its victims—and readers!

Sources

The Tasaday: Stone-Age Cavemen of the Philippines

"First Glimpse of a Stone-Age Tribe." *National Geographic Magazine,* Dec. 1971.

"Anthropologists Debate Tasaday Hoax Evidence." *Science Magazine,* vol. 246: Dec. 1989.

Nance, John. *The Gentle Tasaday: A Stone Age People in the Philippine Rain Forest.* New York: Harcourt Brace Jovanovitch, 1975.

www.uiowa.edu/~anthro/webcourse/lost/tasaday/tasaday.htm

The Great Shakespeare Forgery

Moss, Norman. *The Pleasures of Deception.* New York: Reader's Digest Press, 1977.

Ireland, William. *An Authentic Account of the Shaksperian Manuscripts.* Published online at http://newark.rutgers.edu/~jlynch/Texts/ireland.html

Blundell, Nigel. *The World's Greatest Crooks and Conmen.* London: Hamlyn Press, 1991.

War of the Worlds: A Martian Invasion

Bulgatz, Joseph. *Ponzi Schemes, Invaders from Mars and More Extraordinary Popular Delusions and the Madness of Crowds.* New York: Harmony Books, 1992.

Hadley, Cantrill. *The Invasion from Mars.* Princeton: Princeton University Press, 1982.

www.genericradio.com/waroftheworlds.htm

There's a Sucker Born Every Minute

Saxon, A.H. *P.T. Barnum: The Legend and the Man*. New York: Columbia University Press, 1989.

Sifakis, Carl. *Hoaxes and Scams*. New York: Facts on File, 1993.

Sommer, Robin Langley. *Great Cons and Con Artists*. London: Bison Books, 1994.

www.well.com/user/kafclown/barnum/humbugs.html

Instant Globe-Circling—Just Add Water

Tomalin, Nicholas and Ron Hall. *The Last Strange Voyage of Donald Crowhurst*. Camden, Maine: International Marine/Ragged Mountain Press, 1970.

Roberts, David. *Great Exploration Hoaxes*. San Francisco: Sierra Club Books, 1982.

http://website.lineone.net/~teignmuseum/crowhurst.htm

Operation Bernhard

Pirie, Anthony. *Operation Bernhard*. London: Cassell & Co., 1961.

www.scrapbookpages.com/Sachsenhausen/counterfeit.html

Crazy about Books

Munby, A.N.L. *Portrait of an Obsession*. London: Constable & Co., 1967.

Mitchell, John. *Eccentric Lives and Peculiar Notions*. London: Thames & Hudson, 1984.

Basbanes, Nicholas. *A Gentle Madness*. New York: Henry Holt & Co., 1995.

www.everything2.com/index.pl?node=James%200%20Halliwell-Phillipps

La Grande Thérèse Steps Out

Klein, Alexander. *Grand Deception*. New York: J.P. Lippincott, 1955.

Wade, Carlson. *Great Hoaxes and Famous Imposters*. New York: Jonathan David Publishers, 1976.

Larsen, Egon. *The Deceivers*. London: John Baker, 1966.

John Keely's Good Vibrations

Klein, Alexander. *Grand Deception*. New York: J.P. Lippincott, 1955.

McDougal, Curtis. *Hoaxes*. New York: Dover Publications, 1958.

www.lhup.edu/~dsimanek/museum/keely/keely.htm

The Imaginary Travels of Karl May

Staples, David. "German's Fanciful Stories of Indians Fuel Bizarre Obsessions." *The Vancouver Sun* (Vancouver, B.C.), (date unknown).

Sammons, Jeffrey. *Ideology, Mimesis, Fantasy: Charles Sealsfield, Friedrich Gerstäcker, Karl May and Other German Novelists of America*. Chapel Hill, NC: University of North Carolina Press, 1998.

www.cowboysindians.com/articles/archives/index.html (click on Sept. 1999 issue)

Index

About the Author

Andreas Schroeder's family emigrated from Prussia (today a part of Poland) when he was five years old. As a child, he loved to read. Today, he is the author of more than 20 books of poetry, fiction, and nonfiction and has earned award recognition for his first novel, his nonfiction writing, and most recently for investigative journalism.

Of the many books he's written, *Scams!* is Andreas's fourth on the subject of hoaxes and his first for young readers. For 12 years, he also reported on swindles and deceptions from around the world for a popular national radio program.

Read these other exciting books in the **Stories from the Edge** series

Tunnels! by Diane Swanson

10 gripping true accounts of human drama beneath the ground. Fast-paced and tension-filled, each story propels the reader to the next extraordinary episode.

Escapes! by Laura Scandiffio

History is full of daring escapes. The 10 exhilarating stories in this collection will take readers around the world and across the ages.